WHIPPETS

A PRACTICAL GUIDE FOR OWNERS AND BREEDERS

Pam Marston-Pollock

WHIPPETS

A PRACTICAL GUIDE FOR OWNERS AND BREEDERS

THE CROWOOD PRESS

First published in 2023 by
The Crowood Press Ltd
Ramsbury, Marlborough
Wiltshire SN8 2HR

enquiries@crowood.com
www.crowood.com

British Library Cataloguing-in-Publication Data
A catalogue record for this book is available from the British Library.

ISBN 978 0 7198 4295 5

Cover design by Sergey Tsvetkov

Typeset by Simon and Sons
Printed and bound in India by Parksons Graphics Pvt. Ltd.

Contents

Preface

Whippets have been in my life since 1967, and have given me – along with many people, I'm sure – a great deal of pleasure and have allowed me to achieve much more than I could ever have imagined, not only with successes in the show ring, but also with the opportunity to travel the world as a judge. I have had the honour of judging many beautiful Whippets, and made lifelong friends in many countries.

My intention for this book was to bring to life those early founders of the breed who so often are simply names with their kennel name in brackets. I am therefore indebted to Andy Bottomley and Penny Kastagir, who have shared their family's photos to allow us to see previously unseen images of the Manorley and Balaise Whippets. My thanks to Ciara Farrell and Colin Sealy, from The Kennel Club's library and collections, and Heidi Hudson, curator of The Kennel Club's photographic collections, for their help in sourcing historical material for my research.

Also a special thank-you to Pauline Oliver, who has provided the most stunning photos; and to all those who have contributed other photographs.

I hope this book provides interesting reading and useful information in whatever part a Whippet plays in your life, and that you continue to enjoy them forever!

Pam Marston-Pollock

Acknowledgements

The main photos are by Pauline Oliver; the Manorley photos by kind permission of Andy Bottomley and Penny Kastagir; Pitmen Painters by kind permission of the Ashington Group Trustees. Other photos have been provided by Molly McConkey, Editha Newton, Amy Wilton, Steph Marston-Pollock, Linda Gore, Yulia Titovets, Cath Whimpanny (Harry Whimpanny), Angela Randall and Mary Lowe. Some historical photos are of unknown origin. I would also like to thank Pat Wilson and Sarah Thomas for their pieces on obedience and agility.

The Whippet Breed Standard is the copyright of The Royal Kennel Club Ltd.

I am grateful to have been allowed to use the following photographs by C.M. Cooke: A.H. Opie judging at Crufts in 1951; Paignton Show 1958; Bournemouth Show 1968.

Also the photo by Carol Anne Johnson of Lyn Yacoby Wright and Ch. Cobyco Call The Tune at The Kennel Club with the Crufts Best in Show trophy, along with carved wooden sculptures of Chs. Brekin Spode and Brekin Ballet Shoes.

All are copyright of The Royal Kennel Club Ltd, and are reproduced with The Kennel Club's kind permission.

CHAPTER 1

History and Origins

Over the centuries there have been considerable exchanges between countries, not only in conquests but also in trading. There are different variations of dog that are now established breeds similar to a Greyhound type or 'lévrier' – lévrier being a term given to specialist groups of sighthound or gazehound, that is, hounds that hunt by sight as their primary sense, their quarry normally being the hare or *lièvre*. The word 'lévrier' originates in France. The Whippet is within this group, being a sighthound for chasing hare, or more frequently rabbits. Its origins are not definite, but to look at the Greyhound type is as close to establishing the foundation of the Whippet as we will probably come.

Going back to Roman times, there is no mention of the Greyhound specifically by Xenophon in 300BC. He wrote a *Treatise on Hunting* describing the traditional style of hunting using snares and nets, but two centuries later the 'Greyhound type' was mentioned in the writings of the poet Grattius: 'In a thousand countries you find dogs, each with their own mentality stemming from their origin.' He wrote about the Celts' dogs 'that swifter than thought or a winged bird it runs, pressing hard on the beasts it has found.'

A different type of hunting, that for the pleasure of watching hounds work, was first recognised by Lucius Flavius Arrian, a Roman of Greek ancestry; he was a close friend of Emperor Hadrian (of Hadrian's Wall fame) around 120AD. His knowledge of dogs was extensive, and he was known as 'the younger Xenophon'. He also wrote a *Treatise on Hunting*, and another entitled *Cynegeticus,* books detailing the types of coursing dog, their use and breeding, as well as their training and conditioning. They contain many fine details of traditional ways used by breeders through the centuries with their hunting sighthounds. He highlighted the way in which the hounds used their natural instincts, and, along with Grattius, recognised that the origin of each hound was indicative not only of its mentality but also the style in which it hunted.

His knowledge was drawn from observing both Greek and Roman sports with dogs, and he detailed their different variations: so the Greeks would run a hare along a 'track' made by the viewing public, the Greyhound in pursuit – a type of race more familiar to us today as Greyhound racing – whereas the Roman style was similar to the Whippets many centuries later, where the hare was released in an enclosure and then coursed and caught. Arrian was very empathetic towards his own hounds – he even detailed bringing up his own dog – and named them 'Vertragi'. 'Vertragi' is derived from a Celtic word for 'a powerful but slim dog with a pointed muzzle'. He also kept house dogs, described as 'imported companions for the lady', and Roman miniature Greyhounds.

Roman mosaic showing a Whippet-like hunting dog. (Bardo Museum)

The variations of the lévrier type, or vertragus, spread into many countries of Europe as a result of Celtic culture. These were specific breeds of sighthound, such as Galgos in Spain, Magyar Agar in Hungary, Chart Polski in Poland, and in the British Isles, breeds such as Tumblers, Deerhounds and Irish Wolfhounds as well as the Greyhound. However, it should be noted that there seemed to be no defined breed of Greyhound as such at this time, but more of a Greyhound type of hound. These breeds were bred and developed for hunting, their qualities and abilities 'designed' by the huntsman's needs, and dependent on the terrain and climate of their country and indeed different game. Individually recognised breeds have developed, and although they are unique in their own way, many are genetically related as well as having a generic function – and as with many of them, we will never know their true origins, although modern DNA testing is now beginning to reveal some of their hidden ancestry.

Throughout history, many of these specialist breeds encountered hard times at some time for many different reasons, such as war, famine and disease, as well as the banning of hunting with a lévrier, or hare coursing, all of which resulted in a reduction in numbers, which has periodically threatened those very breeds' survival. The Greyhound type may have provided a useful and typy outcross, not only to boost a breed without introducing uncharacteristic genes, but also, in some cases, to resurrect it. So it is not impossible that many countries have also bred smaller Greyhounds, in effect their own 'Whippets'. The older version of *The Oxford English Dictionary*'s definition of a Whippet is 'a crossbred type of Greyhound'. The Whippet has now been recognised as a breed in its own right for over a hundred years, but has been redefined, with the updated version being 'a small, slender dog similar to a Greyhound'.

Early Mentions in History

The Master of Game, written in 1413 by Edward of Norwich, the 2nd Duke of York, is thought to be the oldest translation of a description of the hunting chase. In Mary Lowe's book *The English Whippet* the following quote describes the advantage of having the right hound for the right quarry: 'The good greyhound shall be of middle size, neither too big he is nought for small beasts and if he were too little he were nought for great beasts.

Nevertheless whoso can maintain both, it is good that he hath both of the great and of the small and of the middle size.' Is he speaking of the early days of the distinct Greyhound, Whippet and Italian Greyhound?

John Caius, also known as Johannes Caius, was an English physician and second founder of the Gonville and Caius College in Cambridge in the sixteenth century, now known as Caius College. He wrote *De Canibus Britannicus*, which identifies many breeds or types of dog, describing their physique and function in great detail. He possibly gives the first mention of a Whippet, but then called a 'Tumbler or Vertragus'. He says:

> This sorte of Dogges, which compasseth all by craftes, frauds, subtelties and deceipts, we Englishmen call Tumblers, because in hunting they turne and tumble, winding their bodyes about in a circle wise...these dogges are somewhat lesser than the houndes, and they be lancker and leaner, beside that they be somewhat prick eared. A man shall marke the forme and fashion of their bodyes, may well call them mungrell Grehoundes if they were somewhat bigger. But notwithstanding they counteruaile not the Grehound in greatness, yet will he take in one day's space as many Connyes as shall arise to as bigge a burthen, and as heavy loade as a horse can carry, for deceipt and guile is the instrument whereby he maketh this spoyle, which pernicious properties supply the places of more commendable qualities.

These first descriptions not only confirm an early existence of the Whippet, but also recognise their working abilities. There were still some writers into the mid-nineteenth century who refused to treat them on an equal footing to other sporting dogs, but some of the first popular dog books eventually did recognise that the popularity of the Whippet warranted mentioning, albeit in less than complimentary words. In the 1879 edition of Vero Shaw's *Illustrated Book of the Dog*, he famously said:

> The Whippet or Snap Dog, as it is termed in several of the Northern Districts of the Country, may scarcely be said to lay down claim to be considered a sporting dog except in those parts, where it is most appreciated. The Whippet is

essentially a local dog and the breed is little valued beyond the limits of the Northern Counties. In these, however, the dog is held in high respect and its merits as to the provider of sport are highly esteemed.

Cultural History

In England, the Whippet has always been described as a 'poor man's Greyhound' or 'poor man's racehorse', stemming from the early 1800s. The workers in the coal-mining communities of the north-east of England, Cumbria, Yorkshire, South Wales and Nottinghamshire, as well as the cotton mill workers of Lancashire and Yorkshire, bred smaller Greyhound types to supplement their food supply as well as providing a sporting pastime such as rag racing or coursing. The Whippet may have no ancient lineage that we can boast of specifically, or none that gives a clear and direct route that the breed has taken through the ages. Certainly in the early nineteenth century there were no pedigrees or other records that show its origin, apart from scant anecdotes.

In fact our breed's heritage is quite modern, and it was the early show-goers who finally gave the Whippet identity. The official recording of pedigrees was not begun until The Kennel Club recognised the breed in 1890. In order to further preserve the Whippet as a specific breed, The Whippet Club was officially registered in 1899. Until this time, many exhibits at shows were of 'unknown' parentage and were often entered as crossbreeds.

The original communities that owned Whippets were working class. The practice of poaching on the landed gentries' estates would, of course, have been illegal, and did nothing for the tarnished reputation of the Whippet – and as a breed, they were frowned upon. Also at this time, coursing with Greyhounds was highly popular, and also lucrative through betting, but was exclusively practised by those whom the poachers probably targeted.

Noted Belgian-born author, Alfred de Sauvenière, himself a landowner near to Paris, introduced coursing meets on his own land, establishing the sport in 1897. A prolific author, his book *Les Courses de Lévriers* (1899) is much sought after. He studied the lifestyle of English coal miners in the latter half of the nineteenth century, and discovered the origins of the sports that became synonymous with the Whippet. It is not surprising that as

a result of de Sauvenière's writings, it became generally accepted that the Whippet originated in the north-east of England. However, this type of rabbit courser was the combination of Greyhound blood with the addition of various breeds or types of terrier, or anything that would enhance their performance in the coursing field. It is thought that Collie was also introduced, and this is reflected in the 'Faults' section of the Whippet Breed Standard. In physique the Collie was strongly muscled and deep-chested, it was generally broken coated, and weighed about 9kg. These dogs would be best suited to the rigorous coursing and catching of live game, and were bred for stamina during a long course.

In around 1875 de Sauvenière also wrote about a fox terrier breeder, John Hammond. Hammond recognised the fine qualities of the 'Greyhound of Italy' that made it a shapely, streamlined runner. He crossed these dogs with his terriers, and produced a racing dog that became extremely successful. Not to be outdone, others quickly followed suit, and this crossbreeding began generations of increasingly whippet-like running dogs with an inbuilt tenacity drawn from the terrier. They were often known as 'Hitalians', and were mainly rough-haired or open-coated. Italian Greyhounds did seem to be a well-established breed in this country by this time, and so presented a useful outcross.

A Variety of Names

Despite being rarely mentioned in renowned books of the dog, where more popular breeds appear, Whippets seem only to be mentioned in descriptions of hunting – but under different names to the Whippet: Rabbit Courser, Tumbler, Rag dog, Snap dog. 'Snap dog' was possibly derived from the other mining areas where the breeds' origin is less appealing. In effectively a course, live prey such as a rabbit was released in a fenced or walled area and the Snap dog gave chase; the dogs were usually used in pairs, and caught their prey with a 'snap!' However, a much more credible source, F.C. Hignett in *The New Book of the Dog* (1907), himself a Whippet 'fancier', said:

A Whippet is too fragile in his anatomy for fighting, so would 'snap' at his opponent with such celerity as to take by surprise even the most watchful, while the strength of his jaw, combined with its comparatively great length, enables him to inflict severe punishment at the first grab. It is owing to this habit, which is common to all Whippets, that they were originally known as Snap dogs.

It is also suggested that 'Snap' comes from the way in which the excited racing dogs snapped at one another, necessitating the development of the racing muzzle. John Caius in his *Canibus Britannicus* had already spoken of Whippets as 'Tumblers', which described the way a Whippet galloped at high speed: full of enthusiasm, stumbling and cartwheeling head over heels, and without breaking rhythm, carried on galloping. This is a trait well known today.

Racing Dogs

Early in the nineteenth century, miners and cotton industrial workers developed 'racing dogs'. These racers were known in Cumbria, Lancashire, Yorkshire and as far south as Staffordshire and West Wales, where racing clubs sprang up as their popularity increased. The racers' appearance indicated that they, too, were bred down from Greyhounds, though their physique was much different to those common in the North East. Firstly they were smooth coated, indicating that they were a purer descendant of the Greyhound, and of lighter build, averaging anything from 5kg up to 10kg. They were much finer and more streamlined in shape. This caused a sport to develop that involved racing the Whippet but without live game; it became very popular as coursing started to lose its appeal and was eventually pronounced illegal.

These racing dogs were of a definite type, because as the sport became more standardised so did the Whippet. The Whippet raced up a straight line of grass or cinder track, up to 150m long, being released at one end either by a handler or latterly from a 'box' or trap, and running towards their owners, who enticed them with treats or waved rags. This racer type was best suited to short, sharp, speed running, much needed to win races. Their appeal also generated an interest in those showgoers of other breeds. They became the foundation stock of the Whippet almost by default, specifically bought in by would-be breeders of the nineteenth century. As their popularity increased, so did those interested in establishing lines that are behind today's show Whippets.

The Whippet in Art

Nineteenth-century Staffordshire inkwells.

There are many works of art, documents and artefacts which show that the Whippet 'type', at least, has been around for some time much earlier than the nineteenth century. Of course it is a breed enthusiast's joy to grab any item where there is a breed likeness evident, and fortunately there is a large array to be had. But looking more into these treasures, the form of a smaller-sized Greyhound can be seen to have origins in other countries of Europe as well as England. A study of the Italian Greyhound by breed researcher Edith Hogel, led her to some of the mummified dogs in ancient Egypt. In a room of embalmed animals, she found a skeleton that showed a strong resemblance not only in shape but also in size to the Italian Greyhound. A larger mummified dog in The Museum of Egyptian Antiquities is of similar type and shape, but much larger in frame. So it is feasible that there could have been a similar dog in between these two in size.

Elsewhere, the famous 'stone dog' of Pompeii is quite Whippet-like in its pose, and in the Vatican Museum in Vatican City many sculptures show a Whippet-like hound. Around the time of the great Low Countries artists, Greyhound types were commonly roaming the streets and feature in many masterpieces.

In many works of art it is questionable as to whether the dog is a Whippet, an Italian Greyhound or a Greyhound. An undeniably close relationship between the three breeds necessitates a difference in 'breed specific' features being recognised, not only those that a breed specialist can recognise, but that are also recognisable to the public eye. This is problematic, as many of

Nineteenth-century English-made life-size bronzes.

the dogs illustrated are not always to scale in relation to the surrounding features. One characteristic for sure is size, which can be estimated by comparison with perhaps his master or surrounding items contained in the work. But it remains that a single work of art can be claimed by a breed enthusiast to be of 'one of theirs', and many works are probably Italian Greyhounds or Greyhounds of varying sizes; however, we can adopt many as illustrating a Whippet.

As we progress into the late nineteenth and early twentieth centuries, a rise in popularity in the Whippet as a breed in its own right generated an interest with artists, who depicted subjects that are clearly Whippets although not titled as such. One painting of great interest to Whippet owners is the portrait of the first two Whippet male champions Zuber and Enterprise from 1892. Painted by William Eddowes Turner, it is owned in a private collection. Modern artists such as Whippet owner Lucien Freud often included Whippets in his paintings.

In the North East of England the famous Pitmen Painters were a group of miners who took up painting

Whippets c.1939 by George Blessed, Pitmen Painter.

as part of the Workers' Educational Association. The art class began on 29 October 1934 in Ashington YMCA hall, and one of its members, George Blessed, painted *Whippets* in 1939. It now hangs in the Woodhorn Mining Museum. Another artist from that area, Norman

Original ink drawing by Eugene Jacobs.

Cornish, whose work has become very popular since his death in 2014, highlights the working man's view of the world and depicts many Whippets in his paintings.

There are contemporary artists within the Whippet community such as Viv Rainsbury, Diana Webber and Bridget Lee, and it is not surprising that the elegance of the Whippet inspired them. The elegant form of the Whippet lends itself to be the model for sculptures, and many are available today in different media. Names such as Nymphenburg, Meissen, Minton and PJ Mene have modelled statues in porcelain, majolica and bronze, and

Twentieth-century model signed PJ 1970.

there are many English models – for example Beswick's model of Ch. Wingedfoot Marksman of Allways, and Border Fine Art's first Whippet model of Falconcrag The Impressario.

Development of 'The Modern Whippet'

In the North East the breed developed more slowly, with the rough-haired variety being more popular – a cross-bred rough-haired working dog that includes Whippet blood can be seen even today. A popular and traditional cross is with the Bedlington Terrier. The rougher-haired Whippet would be more suited to the harsher northern weather as it was probably hardier. As racing gained popularity owners began to shave their dogs, and eventually the smooth-haired predominated.

Early in the nineteenth century, Scottish curator, naturalist and editor Thomas Brown wrote: 'Victorian English writers describe emerging, the modern breed of Whippet or Snap dog, bred for catching rabbits, coursing competitions, straight rag racing and for the novel show fancy.' This is a sudden development, and recognition of the breed as 'the modern Whippet'. Does this intimate that the breed has been elevated from its disreputable past to one of character and type, and become more stylised? The Victorians had a flair for designing many of our present-day breeds, and the Whippet was no exception. For the Whippet to emerge as a show dog as early as the mid-nineteenth century and hold a 'type' must surely support the theory that many communities were breeding to produce a 'breed', and one that was able to fulfil its function and conform to 'standards' – and indeed this would also infer that they had a purity of blood, presumably being bred down from Greyhounds.

One influential Whippet owner, the Duchess of Newcastle, gave Whippets a boost and established the breed within a higher profile. Kathleen, Duchess of Newcastle, lived at Clumber Park in Nottingham and was renowned for her 'of Notts' kennel. She was a leading breeder and respected judge of Clumber Spaniels, Borzois, Smooth and Wire-Haired Fox Terriers, Deerhounds and Whippets. She would probably have been instrumental in drafting Herbert Vickers' letter requesting the recognition of The Whippet Club to The Kennel Club in 1899. Herbert Vickers, the owner of the first Whippet Champion, Zuber, worked as a building contractor along with his father in and around Clumber Park, and this was the address given on his letter to The Kennel Club.

In F.C. Hignett's account of the breed in *The New Book of the Dog* (1907) he says:

> It does not follow that the best-looking Whippet is the best racer, otherwise many of the champion show dogs would never have seen a judging ring in a show, for the majority of them have been disposed of by their breeders because they were not quite fleet of foot enough to win races.

The racing community's loss was certainly the show world's gain. These cast-offs formed the basis on which the modern-day Whippet was built, and many of them continue the legacy and compete successfully at race meetings, as well as being show Whippets.

The Whippet Club was one of the first breed clubs to be registered with The Kennel Club in 1899. The first President was J.R. Fothergill, a Whippeteer, himself recorded as winning Best of Breed at Crufts in 1902 with Trylen Mystery. Early founder officers and committee were B.S. Fitter (secretary); Albert Lamotte of the Shirley kennel; Fred Bottomley, one of the Manorley owners; Lady Arthur Grosvenor, owner of some Ladiesfield Whippets; M. Harding Cox, a member of The Kennel Club; A.H. Opie, a popular judge; W.L. Beara of the Willes' kennel; and J.E. Barker, the first of the Barmaud dynasty. All were influential, playing a part as breeders, exhibitors and judges in the early part of the club's and breed's history, and firmly establishing the breed.

A.H. Opie judging Best Bitch at Crufts in 1951. Second from right, Ch. Shirleymoor Set Fair, who was Best of Breed.

In Herbert Compton's book *Twentieth Century Dogs*, published in 1902, quotes are included from the leading Whippet breeders of the time; they are reproduced here:

… it is pretty certain that the Whippet Club – which now has such names on its front page as Mr J.R. Fothergill, Lady Arthur Grosvenor, Mr Fred Bottomley, Mr Harding Cox, and Mr A. Lamotte – will soon improve the status of the breed, and carry it into the position which the intrinsic merits and physical beauties of the little animal it has been founded to foster, right worthily deserve. The sport of whippet racing suitably conducted is one in which ladies might find a great delight; it offers the quintessence of excitement, crystallised into a few seconds; it is capable of being conducted within private enclosures and kept select, and it adds an attraction to dog-keeping which is not to be obtained in any other breed under the same innocent conditions. There is no blood shed, and there is lots of fun, and, I doubt not, as much joy in owning a winner as in the proprietorship of other 'fleetest of their kind'. And for this reason alone the development of whippet-racing is a consummation which no one could object to.

The following are the notes I have received from my contributors in this section:

Mr J.R. Fothergill (President of The Whippet Club): Nothing could be better as regards type, than many of the bitches now being shown, but the breed requires a few good dogs, a few good breeders, and a few good supporters. The values of the points seem to me good, but in judging by points one can often go wide of the mark. More especially is this the case with whippets and greyhounds. With these dogs individual points are of little importance, even if they have them all in equal perfection, without symmetry, balance and simplicity of construction. The whippet is intended for running only. Many a dog, with a row of bad points, is faster and handier than many a good showing dog. The reason is that they have the above-mentioned qualities.

Judge a whippet out of focus first and then adjust your sight for detail.

I like a whippet first as a race dog, a more interesting study for the subject of animal psychology is hard to find, but there is no need to expatiate upon this somewhat abstract subject here. Like all dogs, their characters are like those of their masters, and they are as easily impressionable, and taught, as any other dog I have had to do with. A thorough bred whippet can be taught retrieving and ratting, whilst he is naturally a better hand at rabbits than a terrier or a greyhound. I have four thorough bred whippets that will hunt the scent of a rabbit or any other scent for any distance. Each takes its own line and they are remarkably clever at casting and travel at a great speed. I have known them to hunt a hare entirely by its scent over the Downs for about a mile and a half. A lady looks better with a whippet than with most other dogs, they are so ornamental. Though if for this purpose a foil is required, a bulldog certainly serves best.

Mr Harding Cox: There is not much fault to find with the type of the breed as it exists today, but breeders must keep up sufficient bone, and must be careful about close, strong, well arched, and well split up feet. I have always judged whippets on greyhound lines, making due allowance for difference of type in hindquarters. Beyond the sport afforded by whippets in sprinting matches and coursing rabbits, I fancy there is little to recommend them as companions, though they are lively and amiable as a rule.

Mrs Charles Chapman: I think there is a danger in breeding whippets fit for the bench only and losing sight of the qualities necessary for racing. The whippet is gifted with extraordinary speed, and for the limited distance it races exceeds that of the greyhound. My bitch Ch Rosette of Radnage accomplished the feat of winning a championship at the Kennel Club Show of 1900, and winning the handicap promoted by the Whippet Club at the same show. Whippet racing, properly conducted, is a most charming sport and essentially suitable for ladies to interest themselves in, and I feel very sorry that the efforts made to popularise it seem to have been without result. Whippets, or more properly speaking race dogs, are capital house companions but their principal interest lies in the sport they afford.

And for my ideal whippet, I see him held in the leash by his handler eager for the start. He is straining every nerve, quivering with excitement and fairly screaming in his anxiety to be after the white rag, to reach which is to the uninitiated the inexplicable cause of this mysterious racing. My ideal is of brindle colour, about 15 or 16 lbs in weight, so that he is well placed in the handicap. His head is long and lean, his mouth perfectly level, his ears small, and shoulders as sloping as possible. His body is well tucked up, with the brisket very deep, his back slightly arched, with a whip tail carried low but nicely curved. His hindquarters are very muscular, and his fore legs absolutely straight, with feet hard and close, and hind legs well turned with hocks bent under him, all the muscles induced by the thorough training he has undergone showing – he looks what he is – a perfect picture of a 'race dog'.

Mr A. Lamotte: The breed is making great strides in the right direction, viz a greyhound weighing about 20 lbs. In the Standard of Points, great value should be laid on power in hindquarters and loin, good feet and legs, deep brisket with plenty of heart room. The whippet was made to race and gallop short distances at a great speed. To see these small pets fighting it out yard by yard on the track is wonderful. And how they love the sport. Unfortunate it is that it is not in better hands, but we must hope that this will improve in time. The whippet as a pet is a very charming animal, and its affection for its owner is great. Watching them running about with their quick graceful movements is a joy to the eye.

Mr Fred Bottomley: The type of whippet today is better than of late, though there is still room for improvement in shoulders, weak pasterns, straight hocks, and size, which in my opinion should not exceed 20 lbs. I am the oldest whippet exhibitor, and for the last ten years have made but few additions to my kennels, always showing my own strain which include Ch Manorley New Boy and Ch Manorley Model, now withdrawn from the show bench. I have always found whippets the best of pals, very game dogs, and the fastest dog living for their size.

This is strong confirmation from the foremost leaders of the breed that the Whippet is firmly established and going from strength to strength. We will probably never know exactly the true origins of the Whippet, but we should be appreciative of these pioneers who clearly had the talent and stockmanship that built such a foundation for the breed that is now one of the most popular.

CHAPTER 2

Early Foundation and Influential Breeders

G.H. Nutt

In the 1893 edition of the Crufts catalogue, George H. Nutt of Pulborough, in Sussex, was recorded as exhibiting five dogs under the heading 'Whippets'. Four of them, entered as 'Pulboro' Tommy, Bluey, Bob and Brindle, were listed as Greyhound/Whippets, while 'Pulboro' Bessy was a Bedlington/Whippet. So it appears that quite a variation would have been present in those early days under the breed heading 'Whippets', and accepted as such. Nutt was well known, distinguished in appearance and very popular with everyone. He raced his dogs as well as showing them, and was famously known for travelling to the Scheveningen show in Holland in the late 1890s with a string of six Whippets. One account of his expedition related that he delighted the dog show people and the Burgomaster with his racing dogs, demonstrating the keenness of Whippets racing – although this was not without its mishaps. He went on to sell many racing Whippets to the Netherlands. George Nutt was also the secretary and show manager of one of the first dog shows at Crystal Palace in June 1870.

Herbert Vickers

For an unusually misty origin, the Whippet has embedded in its history the true founder of the modern Whippet: Herbert Vickers. Whether by his fortuitous link with the Duchess of Newcastle, in the right place at the right time or not, Herbert Vickers' Whippets were well known,

successful, and of a type, and quickly became popular for breeding. The first show champion of the breed, Zuber, was born on 12 April 1889. Bred and owned by the then 26-year-old Vickers, Zuber was to become the foundation Whippet of the breed we have today. Fawn in colour with white collar and trim, he certainly portrays the ideal racing and show dog. Herbert Vickers moved around the Nottingham area during his life as a building contractor, and there are limited accounts of his dogs.

The first mention of Ch. Zuber winning Best of Breed at Crufts was in 1891, along with Vickers' own bitch, Herndell, who was Best Bitch. The judge was George Roper, a well-known judge of the day from Stockton-on-Tees, who wrote descriptions of the Whippet for general information in books, and for the breed introductions in show catalogues. Zuber went on to win at Crufts for another two years, and the entry in the catalogue described him thus: 'Rich brown with white feet and chest, dark muzzle. His general makeup and shape at once strike the eye as being handsome and remarkable. His coat being remarkably fine and not the least bit broken like most Whippets, his weight being 21½lb.'

Herbert Vickers bred a litter born on 18 March 1893 sired by Ch. Zuber, out of Beauty. A male from that litter, Enterprise, became Vickers' second and last champion. Enterprise, a white and fawn male, went on to sire an extremely influential stud dog, Ch. Shirley Wanderer, bred by Albert Lamotte in 1900. Zuber was also used at stud on A.W. Brown's black bitch, Floreat Etona, herself Best of Breed at Crufts in 1894 and 1896.

Ch. Zuber, the very first Whippet champion. Zuber was owned and bred by Herbert Vickers.

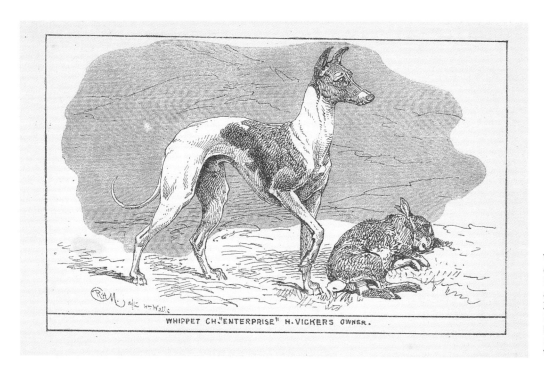

WHIPPET CH."ENTERPRISE" H. VICKERS OWNER.

Victorian engraving of Enterprise, a son of Zuber and Hirondelle, bred by Herbert Vickers.

Herbert Vickers continued to show with some success; at his last appearance at Crufts he recorded that Zuber had won 33 firsts and cups at Crufts. Up until quite recently when entering at Crufts, a 'price if for sale' column appeared on the entry form. In 1892 Zuber was priced at £250, which rose to £500 the following year. However, there is no suggestion that he was ever sold. Herbert Vickers died in 1916, aged 53.

The Bottomley Family

During this period the most influential 'kennel' of pre-war years was making great progress: founded by the Bottomley brothers, the 'Manorley' Whippets began their journey. The brothers were part of the Bottomley dynasty of mill owners in Yorkshire. Their business, S. Bottomley Bros Ltd, started around 1851, in Buttershaw, Yorkshire, and specialised in alpaca and mohair fibre, spinning and manufacturing such goods as luxury suits. The mill still stands today as a Grade 2 listed building. James Bottomley, one of the founders, had a son Thomas who built Manorley Hall, where the kennel name originated. Thomas in turn had a family of seven sons and one daughter, all of whom were involved with dogs. The best known brother in connection with the breed, and possibly one of the main forces behind them being popularised, was Frederick H., or Fred; nevertheless it was a family interest, with at least Algernon, Ernest, James and Clifford being as actively involved, as was their sister, Beatrice Elizabeth Anne.

Bottomley shooting party 1908. Back row, left to right: Jim Hammond, Clifford and Fred Bottomley. Front row, left to right: James, Algernon and Ernest with Chub Bottomley on his knee.

The Bottomley family also had gundogs, Dandie Dinmonts and Greyhounds, a particular favourite of the youngest sibling, Clifford, and Beatrice also kept Italian Greyhounds. They clearly had an eye for spotting show talent in racing Whippets, and regularly purchased stock to add to their kennel; they built a formidable show team, some good enough to be champions in their own right, others bred by the Bottomleys themselves. It is quite probable they had the availability of many Whippets owned and bred by some of their own mill workers.

Throughout their 30 years of breeding and showing, they also sold on dogs for others to show. They established a core of enthusiasts, allowing them also to have the success they were enjoying, but most importantly to broaden the Whippet interest and popularity in the show ring.

Ch. Manorley Model

The first 'Manorley' to gain her title, owned by James and Fred Bottomley, was Ch. Manorley Model, born in 1893, bred by R. Riley. She was the first bitch champion in the breed and was shown with great success, winning at Crufts on three occasions with a total of ten Challenge Certificates.

Model produced Ch. Manorley Toff, who was born in 1898; he was by Ch. New Boy. There is little known of New Boy apart from a photo taken in 1903, although he has a Kennel Club stud book number, and in some articles he carries the Manorley affix. Manorley Marvel, a male from Ch. New Boy and Ch. Manorley May, went on to sire Ch. Esher Toff. Ch. Manorley May was born on 15 June 1899, and was described by Fred Bottomley as follow:

> 17 inches high and 19lbs, grand long head, brown eyes, semi erect ears, small and fine, beautiful neck and shoulders. Her body and legs are perfect and she is framed for speed and work and has proved herself a very fast bitch in handicap races, as well as a great winner on the show bench, she is a prolific winner and highly regarded.

Beatrice Bottomley was married in 1901 to James (Jim) Hammond, himself a prominent, well travelled businessman and accomplished sportsman. His 'contemporary' biography in the West Riding of Yorkshire at the beginning of the twentieth century stated that 'he is the owner

Clifford Bottomley with Greyhounds and a Whippet.

of one of the best Whippet kennels in the world, including Chs New Boy and Manorley Model.' Many family photographs include Jim Hammond, who was particularly interested in gundogs. He showed Pointers, English Setters and Flatcoat Retrievers at Crufts, as well as the Whippets. Around this time Fred moved away from Yorkshire to live on the south coast of England.

Ch. Manorley Maori

One of the most influential sires of those early days, Ch. Manorley Maori, born in 1902, was neither bred nor owned by the Bottomleys. He was bred by a Mr Fowler and owned by a Jesse W. Proctor, but at some time must have been owned and presumably promoted to be a stud dog by 'Manorley' to hold the affix. He also had a former name, Shirley Tramp, so at some time had been in the hands of another successful breeder, Albert Lamotte. Maori was a son of Ch. Shirley Wanderer, himself a grandson and son of the two Herbert Vickers' champions, Zuber and Enterprise respectively. The Bottomleys must have seen the potential in Wanderer and both he and Maori became popular and influential stud dogs. Maori was also a prolific show winner, being awarded ten Challenge Certificates; he was said to be 'a dog of quality, not by any means a big one'.

Apparently there was a similarity in both father and son. Maori was Best of Breed at Crufts in 1904.

Ch. Manorley Mode

Algernon and Ernest Bottomley entered four Whippets at Crufts in 1904: Manorley Mode, Irish Beauty (who had already been a gold medal winner at the Royal Aquarium Show in 1902 for Jim Hammond), Connie Lassie and Mrs Pepper. Ch. Manorley Mode, a bitch born in 1901, bred by W. Smith, was Best of Breed at Crufts in 1905; the silver trophy awarded at that show is still in the ownership of Clifford Bottomley's direct family.

Ch. Manorley Moireen

Fred Bottomley's Ch. Manorley Moireen was probably one of his best and most famous show dogs. Moireen was born on 24 April 1906; she was documented as being formerly named 'Falside Frolic' in one Crufts catalogue, but in the November 1906 edition of The Kennel Club's stud book her registration clearly states that she was bred at Manorley. Often a renaming was done by a new owner to add a kennel's name, but there is no evidence of this, so it is presumed it was a printing error in the catalogue. However, many Manorley

An influential sire,
Ch. Manorley Maori.

Whippets did have their names totally changed. She won her first Challenge Certificate at Crufts early in her puppy career at ten months old, in 1907, and won for the next three successive years; she finally repeated the win again in 1912, but by this time she was owned by Gertrude, Lady Decies. Moireen's sire, Prince George, was quite prolific through his son's line, Ch. Shirley Sunstar.

Two litter brothers, Ch. Manorley Maxim and Ch. Manorley Marco, were bred by Frank Wickett, the founder of the Falside kennel, but he had their names changed to Manorley. They were both owned by Gertrude, the Lady Decies, herself an avid exhibitor in many breeds and other species. Lady Decies also owned Ch. Falside Frivolity, as well as latterly owning Ch. Manorley Moireen. Frivolity had two Manorley parents by Merman from Ch. Mimosa;

she was awarded Best Bitch in Show (All Breeds) at Crufts in 1913. After the death of her husband, Lady Decies met on hard times; she was finally declared bankrupt, having given a loan to a friend for a Golfing Hotel business enterprise that failed. Lady Decies eventually disappeared from the show scene.

Other Notable Manorley Whippets

Frank Wickett of the Falside kennel was an invalid and died in possibly 1911, curtailing early promising years of success as a breeder. He bred Falside Fascination who went on to produce Ch. Delphine for the partnership of Mrs F. Gould and Mr W. Beara as well as producing her full brother, Winstar, who went on to be an important foundation dog for W. Beara's 'Willes' kennel. Ch. Manorley Mimosa stands out for type and quality in her

(Far left) James Bottomley; (second left) Ch. Manorley Moireen shown by Fred Bottomley. (Algernon Bottomley)

photographs, and it is easy to see why she was taken on by Frank Wickett. He bred Chs Manorley Marco, Manorley Maxim and Falside Frivolity, all from Mimosa. She was latterly passed on to Lewis Renwick (Watford) and continued to produce champions for him. Ch. Manorley Magpie, owned by Sir Edmund Chater, was described as white and black as her name suggests, from totally different lines. Bred by T. Oliver, she was born in 1911. Fred Bottomley owned and bred the last pre-war Manorley champion in Ch. Manorley Magnum, a fawn male and son of the prolific Maori.

In 1922, Ernest Bottomley picked up some breeding lines once more and bred the next champion, Fiore, owned by his brother Fred but not holding the Manorley affix: she was out of the unknown 'Lady' but sired by the influential Ch. Willesbeaux, a son of Winstar. Fred Bottomley was described by W. Lewis Renwick as a noted writer on the breed and the doyen of the show Whippet, judging Whippets and Greyhounds at Crufts in 1906.

However, that was not the end of the Manorleys, as one of Fred's brothers, Algernon, had a daughter born in 1910, also named Beatrice Elizabeth Anne. 'Little Bea' was encouraged by her uncle Fred to have an interest in the Whippets and in 1936 she bred a fawn male, Ch. Manorley Manala. He was sired by Ch. Lashaway, owned and bred by J.E. Barker (Barmaud) and out of Harlow Heroine. Manala was owned by Tom Moorby of the famous 'Stainton' kennel, a successful kennel of gundogs, and proved to be influential

and behind many post-war champions from many kennels, but especially when bred to Oxted Dainty Maid.

Dainty Maid was owned by Sam Skelton of the Samema kennel, based in Sheffield. Ch. Samema Dainty Princess and her litter sister Samema Sunray were influential, as Sunray was the dam of the highly acclaimed Ch. White Statue of Cornevan. White Statue was eventually bred to Bea Bottomley's Sporting Chance, and the result was the famous Ch. Brekin Spode. Sam Skelton's Whippets also sparked an interest in a future successful Whippet breeder, Phil Moran Healy (Hillsdown), who as a teenager saw two of Sam's dogs at one of the Sheffield shows and asked him all about them.

'Little Bea' continued through the World War II years under her own kennel name, Balaise, with such dogs as Take Me, Grey Owl, Sporting Chance and Colonel Smasher, who feature in many pedigrees. They went on to be great producers despite not being able to achieve their true show potential due to the war. In 1946, Ch. Balaise Barrie was born, both bred and owned by Bea. Ch. Brekin Spode was bred to Barrie and produced Ch. Brekin Ballet Shoes. Ballet Shoes was purchased from her breeder, Lady Danckwerts, by Dorrit McKay of the famous Laguna kennel. Also in that litter were Brekin Willow Pattern, who went on to produce Chs Fieldspring Bryony, Betony and Bartsia (of Allways) for Lt Col Marengo Jones. Brekin Brown Sugar and Bright Spark also produced champions.

Left to right: Take Me, Sporting Chance, Colonel Smasher and Harlow Heroine.

Family group: top step – Sporting Chance (sire of Silvershoes); middle step – Ch. Balaise Barrie; bottom step – Balaise Beau Geste and Samema Sivershoes (sire and dam of Barrie).

Sporting Chance with Bea Bottomley (Jnr) in 1931 (Watford Sapper Officer ex Harlow Heroine).

Bea Bottomley became a popular judge of Whippets, and Ch. Balaise Barrie won Best Dog at Crufts in 1948. The 'Manorleys', now under the Balaise affix, went on to be the foundation for many important Whippet pedigrees and influential breeders in their own right. Sadly there was only one more litter at Balaise, as once Bea married, she didn't keep any more Whippets from then on. Fred Bottomley was a founder of The Whippet Club and a club official, maintaining his interest in the show Whippet for many years. He continued to attend shows both as a judge and a spectator, and as an official of The Whippet Club. He died on 8 January 1962 aged 89 years back in his native Yorkshire.

Albert Lamotte

As mentioned earlier, at the same time as the Manorleys were showing with such success, a young man, Albert Lamotte, came into the show ring. Born in 1874 in Sydenham, Kent, Albert was in the family tobacco merchant business along with his brother, Lewis, their father having died in 1906. Albert quickly established the Shirley kennel, which got its name from Shirley, near Croydon, where the family lived. He was interested in racing but also had a flair for show dogs, and also kept English Setters and Cocker Spaniels.

He first showed Whippets at Crufts in 1899, exhibiting a bitch, Shirley Pride, who had already won at Crystal Palace in 1898. Pride was later owned by W. Lewis Renwick, being the dam of Ch. Watford Glory and litter sister to Springhill Frivolity. Frivolity was the dam of Ch. Shirley Wanderer, who was Albert's first champion, and a son of Herbert Vickers' Ch. Enterprise. As said earlier, the two most influential stud dogs of the time were Ch. Shirley Wanderer and his son, Ch. Manorley Maori. Maori was originally named Shirley Tramp by Albert; bred from a Shirley dam, he was renamed by the Bottomleys. Albert was establishing a strong line that produced champions such as Watford Glory, Shirley Siren, Shirley Whirlwind and Shirley Sunstar, as well as the continuing line of Manorleys.

Tragedy struck on 21 February 1907, when Albert, aged just 33 years old, and his brother Lewis were drowned when, as passengers on the SS *Berlin*, it was hit by a mine near the Hook of Holland. When floundering, the ship struck the granite backwater when a storm surge wave hit the boat and it sank. Sadly the Shirley kennel was dispersed, and the dogs were taken on by various owners. It would without doubt have been one of the greatest kennels had it not been curtailed so early. It is sad to read the *Kennel Gazettes* of that time and see all the transfers of the Shirley dogs to their new owners. However, it was still the foundation of most of the champions in the pre-World War II years.

W. Lewis Renwick

W. Lewis Renwick became interested in Whippets as a schoolboy and had a lifetime with the breed, becoming an authority, and a successful breeder and judge. His kennel was named 'Watford', and was founded with the help of his father. Born into a renowned family of horse and stock breeders as well as respected judges, Lewis Renwick's cousin, Sir John Renwick, exchanged his homebred 'Springhill Frivolity' for her full sister, 'Shirley Pride', from Albert Lamotte. Pride was later gifted to Lewis Renwick; he described her as 'a big bitch', and an ideal brood bitch. When it was time to breed from her, he was away at school, but he instructed his father to buy a dog journal and find the male with the highest stud fee, which was quoted by Lewis Renwick as being two guineas. The male was Ch. Manorley Maori, and Ch. Watford Glory was born in the resulting litter.

This mating was quite line bred, although it appears this was by chance. Springhill Frivolity and Shirley Pride being full sisters, Frivolity was the dam of Ch. Shirley Wanderer, who in turn was the father of Ch. Manorley Maori. Lewis Renwick went on to produce a most successful line, with Ch. Watford Brilliant proving to be a popular stud dog, himself closely line bred to Ch. Shirley Wanderer and therefore Ch. Enterprise and Springhill Frivolity. As mentioned previously, Lewis Renwick also latterly owned Ch. Manorley Mimosa, who had been in the ownership of Frank Wickett (Falside); she was a lovely typy bitch and became a great producer, and, along with many Watfords, provided the basis for many kennels.

W.L. Beara

Willie Beara founded his kennel in 1912. He has an outstanding record of Whippet champions but not all bearing the Willes affix. He began with the foundation bitch

THE WHIPPET CLUB

(FOUNDED 1899)

President : W. LEWIS RENWICK

Hon. Secretary : E. J. SOBEY

SCHEDULE

OF AN

OPEN SHOW FOR WHIPPETS

(*Under Kennel Club Rules and Show Regulations in force at date of publication of this Schedule*)

will be held at

THE LONDON SCOTTISH DRILL HALL,
BUCKINGHAM GATE, LONDON, S.W.

ON
THURSDAY, 15th NOVEMBER, 1945

Judging commence at 2 p.m. prompt.

Judge :
J. E. BARKER, ESQ., Huddersfield.

Guarantors to the Kennel Club :
E. J. SOBEY, ESQ., Cotehele, Truro.
J. E. BARKER, ESQ., The Kennels, Fennay Bridge, Huddersfield.
W. LEWIS RENWICK, 4, Western Avenue Court, Llandaff.

Show Committee :
Messrs. W. L. RENWICK, E. J. SOBEY, J. E. BARKER (Hon. Treasurer)

Stewards :
Mrs. C. A. MARTIN, Miss B. C. A. BOTTOMLEY, Messrs. B. S. FITTER, EMLYN OWEN, ROBERT BARRY and E. BURGESS.

Hon. Veterinary Surgeon :
C. H. BRYANS, M.R.C.V.S., Parkstone, Dorset.

Dog Show Manager and Secretary :
W. L. RENWICK, Red Holme, Llanbethery near Barry, Glam.
'Phone : St. Athan **95**.

THIS SHOW WILL **NOT** BE BENCHED.

ENTRIES CLOSE : MONDAY, 5th NOVEMBER (Postmark)

Front cover of The Whippet Club schedule for the 1945 show, showing the founders of The Whippet Club.

Falside Fascination from Frank Wickett's kennel, and had a flair for quality. One of his most important stud males was Willesberg, who headed an influential stud force of valuable males. Willie Beara served as the president of The Whippet Club for some time; C.H. Douglas Todd wrote a tribute to him in his book *The Popular Whippet*, describing him as a perfect gentleman who truly had the breed at heart. Beara seemed to be very modest as to his success, but as Douglas Todd said: 'Kindly, helpful, full of fun and good spirits, he was without doubt one of the greatest hearted doggy men I have ever known.' In his view Willie Beara would have been an excellent judge, but he refused to officiate in the ring; when asked why not, he said: 'Well, old friend, you know how they take it to heart – why make them unhappy?'

Stanley Wilkins

There is one more kennel worthy of particular note from this era and that is Stanley Wilkins' Tiptree kennel, taking its name from the fruit preserve family business. Having bred only three champions carrying the Tiptree affix, although none were owned by him, he was known for not particularly presenting his dogs well for a show. There is a considerable amount of Tiptree in pedigrees in the 1930s. Stanley Wilkins bred a large number of Whippets, their background being drawn from the Manorley, Shirley and Watford lines, and these were used extensively by breeders looking to line breed.

He himself line bred to a male, Ch. Towyside Tatters, who had five lines to Ch. Shirley Wanderer. At that time sometimes under a certain amount of criticism for his close inbreeding regime, C.H. Douglas Todd recognised 'he has certainly improved the fronts and feet within the breed, and size he seems to have completely mastered – and the one thing about the Tiptrees, they are certainly a level lot'. A phrase still used today by breeders recognising a consistency of type.

Influential Breeders and Bloodlines

The legacy of those early breeders meant that a positive nucleus of Whippets was able to pass on their virtues, and as more interested enthusiasts brought their talents to the breed, a strong foundation was laid and Whippets became a force to be reckoned with, especially in the show ring. Interesting reading in both W. Lewis Renwick's *The Whippet Handbook* and C.H. Douglas Todd's *The Popular Whippet* gives first-hand accounts of the next generation of breeders who utilised these lines and produced the many champions that are now disappearing from the edge of pedigrees. They write in a very conversational way and give many personal accounts of how the Whippet world was during these years.

Following the end of World War II, the growth of Whippets in the show ring was substantial and a new era of breeders began establishing their own lines. Most picked up lines from these foundation kennels. As breeders, they began their quest not only to preserve the breed type, but also to put their own stamp on the breed. In these progressive times there was probably a much more even type in general – many photos of those Whippets are very similar in head type, body shape and colour. Whippet bloodlines began to be focused on a few successful dogs of the day, and in hindsight the breed was fortunate, as they were dominant and good producers. It just needed talented breeders with foresight to carry these lines for our benefit.

There have been many great producing kennels since these early days, which have gone on to influence the path the breed has taken; they are too many to mention in detail, but they have contributed in keeping the Whippet true to type, and just as importantly, true to their function. Moving from the 1950s, Brekin, Wingedfoot, Peppard of Test, Allways, Ladiesfield, Ballagan, Dragonhill, Fleeting, Seagift, Wingedfoot, to name but a few, were all highly successful. During the 1960s and 1970s, the breed enjoyed the talents of many notable breeders who had built their breeding lines on those foundation kennels. Important kennels emerged that established a breeders' type, which became instantly recognisable from the ring side.

Dorrit Mckay

The Laguna Kennel of Dorrit McKay was one of these important kennels. In 1939 Dorrit and her husband travelled to Essex to view a horse, and whilst they were in the area, decided to call on Stanley Wilkins. Tiptree Joan became the first Whippet at Laguna. Breeding down from Joan, Ch. Tiptree Jay was owned by the Seagift kennel, and Jay's litter sister was in turn bred to Ch. Sapperley Heralder. The first champion to hold the Laguna affix was Laguna Liege. Liege was said to be 'less than

Ch. Wingedfoot Marksman of Allways, a popular and dominant stud dog owned by C.H. Douglas Todd.

eyecatching when standing, but moved like a thoroughbred horse', winning his first Challenge Certificate whilst still quite young towards the end of 1949. He was Best in Show at The Whippet Club Jubilee Show in March 1950, becoming a champion two months later.

In 1952 Dorrit bought Brekin Ballet Shoes, then aged two years old, from Lady Danckwerts, and this bitch proved to be the most valuable foundation for a long line of Laguna champions: Laguna Lullaby, Lily of Laguna, Limelight, Linkway, Leading Lady, (Greenbrae) Laguna Lucia, Light Lagoon, Leisure, Laguna Porthurst Moonlight Sonata, Laguna Ravensdowne Astri and Lunanute. Dorrit had the foresight to bring together many of the breed's foundation lines, and for 60 years has been revered not only in the show ring but also in racing and coursing circles, earning worldwide recognition. Her most influential male was undoubtedly Ch. Laguna Ligonier. Born in 1960, Ligonier sired eleven champions in the UK alone. He was dual purpose, often coursing on a Thursday, shown on a Saturday and raced on a Sunday. Dorrit McKay was a leading influence on the modern-day Whippet in all disciplines. This was possible because she bred Whippets that were noted for speed, stamina and elegance. Ligonier not only sired champions, but his daughters also produced them.

During her 38 years with the Whippet Coursing Club, Laguna ran 54 Whippets, 32 of them being finalists 175 times, winning 75 stakes and dividing or being runner-up 100 times. At least 200 coursing Whippets have had a Laguna sire or dam. Laguna has won the Moonlake Cup for Top Coursing Dogs with six males, of which two have won it twice. Not to be outdone, the Laguna Cup for Top Coursing Bitches has been awarded to twelve Lagunas, several of them winning twice.

Alongside the Laguna kennel, dual purpose Whippets held their own within the show rings as well as in the field. Two of the best known are Mary Lowe's Nimrodel and Gay Robertson's Moonlake Whippets. Their contribution to the breed is, and remains immeasurable, and both are well respected throughout the dog world.

Mary Lowe

Mary Lowe is one of the breed's authorities and author of *The English Whippet*. She bred many Nimrodel champions in the show ring, and her Whippets were also successful in the coursing and racing world. Mary was a long-time committee member of The Whippet Club and

Left to right: Mrs Yerborough with Ch. Greenbrae Laguna Lucia, R.M. James (Samarkands), and Ch. Laguna Ligonier with Dorrit McKay, one of the most prolific producers of champions of his time.

Mary Lowe (Nimrodel), a most respected breeder and judge and doyen of the breed.

The Whippet Coursing Club, and acted as registrar for the Whippet Club Racing Association; she was also a talented racehorse breeder. Her opinion was much sought after all over the world as a judge, but her knowledge on the development of the Whippet Breed Standard meant that her talks were always extremely well attended. Regarded as the doyen of the breed, her numerous champions were all carefully bred to established fawn lines, and were very recognisable in the show ring. She also had a line that produced colours, and campaigned blacks to their titles. The Nimrodels are famous for their adaptability both in the show ring and in the field.

Gay Robertson

Gay Robertson is a popular and well known judge and exhibitor, but her prowess is in producing the dual-purpose 'Moonlake' Whippets. A long-time official of The

31

Whippet Club, and a panel member of The Kennel Club's publication *The Kennel Gazette*, she regularly writes features on many different breed disciplines and topics. She owned the celebrated dog Moonlake, not only a WCRA champion, but he also won the Nicholl Trophy on three successive seasons in the coursing field. By winning the trophy outright, it was renamed the Moonlake Cup (as already mentioned as being won by Laguna dogs). Her Whippets regularly compete in lure coursing competitions both here and in Europe, and she is also a regular exhibitor in the show ring.

Showing Success

Several Whippets began to have great success not only at breed level, but also achieving Championship Show Group and Best in Show wins, none more so than in the last forty years. To mention a handful of kennels seems so inadequate in such a numerically strong and popular breed, but these kennels had such an influence on the future development of Whippets because of the quality stock they produced, and also by way of introducing new enthusiasts, who themselves went on to establish their own lines and become successful in their own right.

Barbara Wilton-Clark

The Shalfleet kennel, piloted by Barbara Wilton Clark, was always a force to be reckoned with. It was built on its first few brood bitches, namely Ch. Shalfleet Brandy of Selbrook and Wingedfoot Bartette. Strong lines back to Ch. Wingedfoot Marksman of Allways and Ch. Fieldspring Bartsia of Allways in turn produced the first of Barbara's four champions in three years. She produced a long line of champions, not only Whippets but also some fabulous Greyhounds. She had a flair for producing top quality hounds, and was highly competitive in the show ring but was also willing to help and encourage others. One of her outstanding bitches is used to illustrate the Breed Standard: Ch. Sequence of Shalfleet, a true 'English Whippet'.

At the time, importing Whippets into the UK was not a regular occurrence due to quarantine restrictions, but Barbara saw a need for some fresh bloodlines and imported Samoem's Silent Knight of Shalfeet, who quickly became a champion and went on to produce consistently good litters. Barbara is now retired from

showing and breeding, but continues as a well-respected judge. Her daughter Jane has continued the kennel's success, and Ch. Shalfleet Simply A Lord is the current male breed record holder.

Bill and Anne Knight with Bobby James

Bill and Anne Knight were originally interested in racing Whippets. They had a lifetime's friendship with R.M. (Bobby) James, himself a successful Whippeteer who held the Samarkand kennel name, and latterly one of our top multibreed judges; this friendship began a dynasty of Dondelayo and Samarkand champions. This kennel specialised in line breeding and produced many champions, not only for themselves but first champions for many future breeders. The most influential sire, Ch. Samarkand's Greenbrae Tarragon, born in 1961, revolutionised their lines and proved to be a great producer. All were Laguna bred with lines back to Marksman and the Brekin bitches. Whippets such as Ch. Dondelayo Buckaroo, and a famous bitch line of champions Rue, Roulette, Duette, Reinette, Ruanne, Dyanne and Tiara formed the foundation for successful kennels such as the Meakin's Oakbark, Roma Wright-Smith's Silkstone, Roger Stock's Courthill, and Glenbervie, owned by Arthur Badenoch Nicolson.

Glenbervie

Originally with an interest in gundogs, Arthur Badenoch Nicolson soon established a valuable breeding stock of Whippets, and none more influential than Ch. Cockrow Tarquogan of Glenbervie. Bred by sisters Anne and Elizabeth Hudson (Cockrow) and little shown by them, Tarquogan, born in 1963, was a Tarragon son and joined his father in being one of the great producers of the time. Arthur bought Tarquogan and used him on Ch. Hillgarth Sunstar of Glenbervie and White Gorse of Glenbervie, and Anne Knight used him on Ch. Dondelayo Rue: these alliances produced nine champions in total. Glenbervie provided first breed champions for Jack Peden's Denorsi kennel and my own Falconcrag kennel, while White Bud of Glenbervie, owned by Phil Moran Healy's Hillsdown kennel, and many Glenbervie bitches, were the foundation of now famous Whippet breeders.

Paignton Show in 1958: Mrs M. Wigg with Ch. Ladiesfield Starturn (left), (centre) judge Leo Wilson, Miss D. Cuzner with Bellavista Fern, who was Best of Breed.

Bournemouth Show in 1968: Mrs A. Argyle and Ch. Harque the Lark (left), (centre) judge Mr Stan Kay, Mrs Molly Garrish with Ch. Fleeting Flamboyant. The Lark was Best of Breed.

Jane Wilton-Clark's Ch. Shalfleet Simply A Lord, the Male Breed record holder.

Barmoll

Molly McConkey had an early interest in the breed, and began her career as a junior handler in 1956, showing two Whippets, both by the famous 'Marksman'. After a period out of the ring she restarted with Brandy Smash of Barmoll, registering her affix in 1975. The first litter produced from Brandy Smash was to Garnstones Nearco of Shalfleet, which was line bred to Marksman. This produced the stunning Ch. Barmoll Beelzeebub. She went on to produce the lovely fawn Ch. Barmoll Beejapers, who proved her worth as a brood bitch with four UK champion children. She was the top brood bitch in 1991 and 1993, with her offspring winning both the Dog and Bitch CCs at Crufts in 1993. Surely one of her most satisfying days was at The Whippet Club of Wales Championship Show in 1991. Both the Dog and Bitch CC winners, and the reserve Dog CC winner were from Beejapers, as were the Best Dog and Bitch puppies – and Beejapers herself was Best Veteran in Show. What a record! This is undoubtedly the mark of a talented breeder, and the Barmolls continue to produce lovely Whippets today.

Oakbark

The Meakin Family have had a long association with Whippets, and with their first champion Oakbark Dondelayo Storming they soon became established, known across the world for their breeding and showing talents. Oakbark is one of the top kennels, with over thirty champions, piloted for many years by Dennis Meakin in the show ring, a familiar face to all. Some of the loveliest bitches were from Oakbark – such as Mariel, Must Love and Movie Queen – and their stud dogs were a valuable asset to the breed, including Ch. Oakbark Middleman, owned by Phil Moran Healy. One dog that is most worthy of mention is Ch. Oakbark Millenium Gold. Now Dennis and Dorothy's daughter Julie and granddaughter Sarah continue the legacy.

Hillsdown

Phil Moran Healy had an early interest in the breed and later came to establish one of the most influential kennels. His talent for breeding brought together some of the best

The Whippet
Club of Wales
show in 1991:
left to right:
Molly McConkey
with Ch. Barmoll
Blaze of Gold,
Mary Rigby with
Ch. Barmoll
Blackthorn,
Betty Beaumont
with Ch. Barmoll
Beaujolais at
Teisanlap.

Molly
McConkey's
Ch. Barmoll
Beejapers, top
brood bitch in
1991 and 1993.

Ch. Moonlight Model at Oakbark and Ch. Oakbark Master Cobbler with Julie and Dennis Meakin and judges Mary Lowe (Nimrodel) and Lucinda Aldrich-Blake (Astrophel) in 1994 at the Hound Association Championship Show.

bloodlines, which formed the basis not only for his own success, but as a secure foundation for the breed in general. His kennel was based on Glenbervie lines through Denorsi stock. There are many important dogs that carry the Hillsdown lines that have proved their worth, not only in the show ring but more importantly as breeding stock, and not only here, but in many countries across the world. As regards making up champions, Phil is one of the best respected breeders and judges. A string of lovely Hillsdown champions were headed by the male Hillsdown Fergal, who although not gaining his title, proved to be an important influence on the breed; he sired the famous BIS Crufts winner, Ch. Pencloe Dutch Gold.

Dumbriton and Courthill

Two of the most popular breeders and exhibitors are Patsy Gilmour (Dumbriton) and Roger Stock (Courthill).

They have been lifelong friends, and have worked in a partnership that has produced and campaigned some of the best Whippets. They have never shied away from importing new lines and helping many exhibitors with quality Whippets. Patsy's influential male Ch. Lowglen Cavalier was a prolific stud dog, and produced the lovely Eidelweiss, amongst many others. Patsy has always been forward thinking, introducing different bloodlines, and has crafted their bloodlines to continue an unequalled path of success. Her talent for presenting her Whippets in the ring is unchallenged.

Roger has produced many champions in many countries as well as the UK under his own affix Courthill, originally based on Shalfleet bloodlines. He continued by introducing Ch. Courthill Dondelayo Tiara, and also bred Ch. Courthill Coronet and Crown of Gold. Patsy and Roger's Ch. Courthill Cast A Shadow was Best of Breed at Crufts in 2009, judged by myself. Both Patsy and Roger are popular international judges.

Patsy Gilmour (Dumbriton), one of the breed's expert handlers of many lovely champions.

Roger Stock (Courthill) with Ch. Courthill Cast A Shadow.

Nevedith

Established by Nev, Edith and Editha Newton, this kennel has had an unprecedented amount of success for more than forty years in the breed. Nevedith is the most successful kennel in the UK, producing champions and foundation stock for many breeders worldwide. Their first litter was born in 1967 from two 'Harque' parents, both bred by Ann Argyle: Harque to Beaumont and Harque to Infanta, owned by Editha, as with all the Nevediths. I can remember during a visit to Nevedith that Nev was eager to show a puppy he had purchased, brindle with white trim, later to become Ch. Akeferry Jimmy. Jimmy was a double great grandson of Ch. Laguna Ligonier as well as a great grandson and grandson respectively of Ch. Samarkands Greenbrae Tarragon, as mentioned earlier, two of the breed's most influential sires.

Jimmy was to prove true to his pedigree and became one of the most prolific sires himself, producing the base

Edith and Nev Newton: along with their daughter Editha, founders of the famous Nevedith Whippets.

on which Nevedith Whippets were founded. His pedigree was matched to bitches carrying lines to Tarragon; one such bitch was Ch. Skytime of Glenbervie, a double granddaughter of Ch. Cockrow Tarquogan of Glenbervie, himself a Tarragon son. This mating produced Ch.

Ruegeto Nina of Nevedith. Over time, Jimmy was used on a number of bitches who carried similar lines, as did the Glenbervie, Cockrow, Tantivvy and Dondelayo bitches.

One Jimmy daughter, Nevedith April Mist, was mated to Akeferry Admiral, a son of Ch. Baydale Cinnamon (a grandson of Tarragon and Cockrow Mayday, a Tarragon daughter). This produced Ch. Nevedith Bright Beret, owned by Ray Hill, and he was mated to a daughter of Nina, producing Ch. Nevedith Hill Breeze. Ray Hill also owned Ch. Crysbel Skylight of Nevedith, another Jimmy daughter: she was from the lovely Ch. Crysbel Skylark, a daughter of Ch. Fleeting Fulmar, whose dam Akeferry Miss Emma was Jimmy's litter sister.

Ch. Huntress of Nevedith was a Jimmy great grand-daughter through her sire Ch. Harque to Huntsman, and dam, Night Star of Nevedith. Ch. Nutcracker of Nevedith, campaigned in the mid-1970s, was another combination of Jimmy, this time to White Bud of Glenbervie, a Tarquogan granddaughter. He was bred at Hillsdown by Phil Moran Healy, and was one of the first successful males since Jimmy. Ch. Nevedith Paperweight was top stud dog in 1985, his most notable progeny being out of a Jimmy daughter: Uptown Guy, Up at the Top and Up Sadaisy all gained titles worldwide.

Ch. Nevedith Uptown Guy's dam Sakonnet Alf Alfa was another Jimmy daughter, out of Sakonnet Black Mustard, whose dam Ch. Sakonnet Sprig Muslin was herself a Jimmy daughter. Uptown Guy mated Chilka Dairy Maid, owned by the Barkers. Dairy Maid, a daughter of Pearl of Akonyte (also bred by Phil Moran Healy), was mated to Ch. Oakbark Middleman, thus bringing together a concentration of lines to Tarragon, but equally the strong influence of the Hillsdowns.

Ch. Nutshell of Nevedith, the most famous of this litter, is the current breed record holder. Nutshell was Reserve Best in Show at Crufts, and she was mated to the Crufts Best in Show winner Ch. Pencloe Dutch Gold, who became one of the most influential sires of our time. His pedigree, that of a dominant stud dog, brought together with Nutshell's strong bitch line, proved to be the classic textbook pedigree.

Meanwhile, Nevedith Victory Salute was mated to Ch. Maximillian of Carmodian, a Merry Monarch daughter, bringing together two lines to Ch. Baydale Cinnamon;

Ch. Nevedith Zippy Zimmer was himself a colourful brindle. Ch. Nevedith Yo Ho-O from Novacroft was a son of Sakonnet Alf Alfa and Neeko of Nevedith, a grandson of Jimmy and Paper Weight.

In 1993 the litter brother and sister Chs Nevedith Justa Jesta and Justa Jenie from the Dutch Gold–Nutshell litter made their debut and quickly gained their titles. Jenie gained her first two CCs as a minor puppy, and made up early in 1994 losing out for BOB to Jesta, who had just won his first CC.

Jesta sired Ch. Pardee Appy Arry of Nevedith (who in turn sired Ch. Nevedith Quality Quire of Loroli) and Ch. Nevedith Upperly Uppercrust at Dunaruna and Jesta's litter sister, Justa Joy, produced Ch. Nevedith Xfa Xtacy at Marchpast. Joy was also the dam of Ch. Nevedith Rare Rogue. Rare Rogue was mated back to Jenie to produce Ch. Nevedith Veefa Vesper at Marchpast and Ch. Nevedith Veffa Vanity at Roguesmoor. He also sired Ch. Nuts in May of Nevedith.

A repeat mating of Dutch Gold and Nutshell in 1994 produced the brindle bitch Ch. Nevedith Major Mystery. Mystery was mated to Peperone Passat; their daughter, Ch. Nevedith Teefa Tuppence was owned by the Coopers. In 2000, a litter was born from Ch. Nuts in May of Nevedith to Ch. Whipcat Fire Island at Courthill; Fire Island brought some new blood-lines through Sporting Fields Jazz Fest but also US and Canadian Ch. Nevedith Justa Jigsaw. Two males, Ch. Nevedith Ayfa Aze and Ch. Nevedith Ayfa Ayrik, gained their titles in 2002. Nuts in May was then mated to Jesta, and Ch. Nevedith Efa Empra and Ch. Nevedith Efa Empress were the result.

One breeder, Rob Bailey (Fullerton) saw the potential in Jesta and latterly Rare Rogue to complement his lines, and produced six champions directly. Ch. Fullerton Dream Mover, a Rare Rogue son, was mated back to Nuts in May and produced Ch. Nevedith Kfa Kracka; he in turn sired Ch. Nevedith Mfa Markwiss at Marimay and Ch. Nut Chip of Nevedith. Another line to Jazz Fest was introduced, Ch. and Int. Ch. Rivarco Classic Jazz, whose dam Rivarco First Lady was herself a daughter of Nevedith Justa Joker and Nevedith Fire Glow. Classic Jazz was mated to Efa Empress, producing Ch. Nevedith Lfa Lady Love.

Ch. Nevedith Yehfor Yasmin has a pure Nevedith pedigree: her sire was Nevedith Boxing Helena's Justaking, an Empra son from Int. Ch. Nevedith Pfa

The Whippet breed record holder Ch. Nutshell of Nevedith.

Princess, a Kracka daughter. Recognising the true potential of their stock, and having the clear foresight and talent for careful selection, combined with the flair for presentation in the show ring, is no mean feat. Sadly, in 2018 we lost two-thirds of Team Nevedith when Nev and Edith passed away. But it is a fitting tribute to them that this long line of champions is part of the breed's history.

In Conclusion

As mentioned earlier, it is nigh on impossible to include all the very talented breeders who continue the legacy and breed very special Whippets. I consider the above to be the 'middle generation' who picked up the mantle and continued the breed, strengthening the gene pool to enable their followers to maintain the breed.

CHAPTER 3

Choosing a Breeder

You have made that important decision: you would like to welcome a new member to your family, a Whippet. Notice I said a new member to your family, not just a dog, but a pet that will become very much part of your family. It is important that you have considered what this means, especially if you haven't had a dog in your household before. You should be aware that this Whippet could be a part of your lives for the next fifteen years or so. Why would you like a Whippet – is it purely as a companion, or would you like to do some of the many activities available?

Does your lifestyle have room for your Whippet? Do you have a secure, fenced garden or outside area? Would you be able to give sufficient time to your pet? If you go out to work, how long will it be left alone, or can you afford doggy day care? Can you afford good dog food, especially when the puppy is growing, or unexpected vet bills and/or pet insurance? Your Whippet will need walking every day, a minimum of twice a day without fail, no days off. Will all your family be comfortable with a dog in the family home? Would you mind muddy paws on your floor or furniture? If you want to go on holiday, will your Whippet come too, or what arrangements will you need to make?

These are just a few questions that need careful consideration before you embark on a search for a puppy. Be prepared to answer, at least, most of these questions from the breeder of your prospective puppy, and consider whether you would prefer to have a male or female. A male can be affectionate and loving and makes a very good pet, whereas a female can have a stronger will and can often be more independent.

Seeing a breeder's adults gives an idea of how the puppies will look when they are full grown.

Rescue Whippets

There are Whippets that are looking for homes as rescues. The basic questions are still as relevant, and in addition to finding out the age and history of the rescue Whippet, any reputable rescue organisation should be able to give you details outlining their temperament and habits. This may have had a bearing on the reason the Whippet is in a rescue situation in the first place, so it is important you ask those questions. The rescue organisation should already have done an assessment on the rescue Whippet, which would establish its personality and highlight any issues that exist – you may be taking on a dog with problems, both health and behavioural. Not that this should particularly put you off, but you really need to be aware of those issues, so you are well prepared and fully understand what you are taking on.

It would be helpful to know if the Whippet is purebred, as far as is possible. Sometimes it can happen that a rescue 'Whippet' puppy can grow and grow, and is in fact nearer to a large Greyhound when fully grown. There are many cross-bred Whippets around that look correct as puppies, but take on other characteristics as they develop into adults.

Whilst this is a rewarding way of giving a home to a Whippet, it requires you making a decision from the head, not just the heart. The rescue centre will do checks to see if they consider you and your home are suitable. You will be asked, probably in an interview-type situation, all sorts of questions: these can range from the facilities you have at home, to the time that you can spend with your rescue every day. How would a rescue impact on the rest of your family? How much time can you devote to possibly retraining your rescue if it is 'uneducated', or dealing with health issues that may already be there or may crop up later? Are you prepared for extra, unexpected vet bills? …and so on. The rescue dog will have been neutered, or you will be required to have this done.

Giving a home to a rescue Whippet can be an excellent way of finding the right dog for you, but be prepared to walk away if you don't feel it is, and never feel sorry for it – the dogs in these centres are well looked after. One organisation dedicated to rehoming Whippets is the JR Whippet Rescue Organisation established by Joanna Russell over fifty years ago. It has many experts available to help you make the right choices, and they often have a number of Whippets requiring permanent homes.

How do you choose? This quality puppy is a good example of one to consider.

Buying a Puppy

If you decide that a puppy is the best option for you, it is important to do your homework before rushing into a purchase. Earlier we mentioned the activities, if any, that you would like to do with your Whippet. Some new owners have a clear idea of what they would like to do, but often this comes about by accident, by meeting others with an interest, hearing about it and thinking of 'having a go'. However, this may have a bearing on where you decide to look for your Whippet puppy – although a Whippet is very adaptable, and will often enjoy participating in an activity to achieve different levels, irrespective of the role it has been bred for. For instance, a racing whippet is often bred specifically with that in mind, and a show-bred whippet is bred for looks, while a rescue dog may be of 'unknown' parentage. However, whatever the purpose they were originally bred for, they should have the potential to be a lovable pet for you, and would probably adapt to anything you wanted to do with them, up to a certain level.

Spend some time doing your research, and go to watch racing or lure coursing or other activities at organised events. Many clubs run events that you can attend – a good place to start is 'Discover Dogs', run by The Kennel Club. They run two events during the year, where you can speak to breed experts who can answer all your questions, as they themselves own Whippets and take part in many of the disciplines. You can also meet Whippets of different types, and can obtain extensive information in the form of handouts. To begin with, you will find it beneficial to speak to as many people as possible about the breed in general, and to get a feel for the look of the dogs; most enthusiasts are happy to spend time giving advice without being pushy about selling you a puppy. Ask about the availability of future puppies and inquire as to the cost.

Go home and discuss with your family what you have found. Have a look on The Kennel Club website for registered breeders who are members of the Assured Breeders Scheme. Each breeder has had an inspection visit and has obligations to fulfil before they can be assured, so this is a good option.

When you have come to a decision about the kind of Whippet that is best suited to you, then go back and look again. For instance, there may be a certain colour or type you like. It is always possible that breeders have puppies available that will not be of the quality or showing promise that they are looking to keep, and the price may vary – just like the racing dogs that were sold to the show goers in the early days because they weren't fast enough!

Whippets come in many colours, and it is down to personal preference which colour you would like. All colours or combinations of colours are typical. There is cream and fawn, and these two colours come in a variety of shades from the palest cream to the darkest red fawn. There is brindle, which can vary from the lightest lemon-coloured background to a dark red background, with either black or blue stripes as an overlay. There is black or blue (a steely grey colour). Whippets of these colours may also have a white trim on their face, neck, legs and feet, or they may be solid coloured. White also comes as a solid colour, or as a particolour – that is, mainly white on the body with patches of any of the above colours. This is not as common as the main colours, but is very popular when they do occur.

It should be noted here that blue merle, a colour seen in some other breeds, is not genetically possible in the purebred Whippet, and has been linked to health issues in other breeds, so if you do come across this colour in a Whippet puppy, it should be avoided completely.

Meeting the Breeders

Choosing a breeder with whom you feel comfortable is extremely important. They should not be pushy in making a sale, but should spend time with you to establish that a Whippet is the right puppy for you, and more importantly that you are the right owner for their puppy! They should be happy to send you photos of the puppies and close relatives; often they have a website to view.

There are different kinds of dog breeder, and it is worth being aware of the differences as it may affect the quality and health of your puppy. A breeder who has one or two

The breeders' adults should be happy and content.

litters a year and has the breed at heart will be pleased to answer any questions and should be open about all aspects of their dogs. They should be able to show you pedigrees, photos, even prize cards from shows or other events, and should be visibly proud of their achievements, and more importantly their Whippets. The Whippets by their very nature will be totally at ease and comfortable in and around their owner, and will interact well with the rest of the family.

In contrast, a breeder who is just out to make a few pounds will not show the same interaction with their Whippets, and vice versa; they may be abrupt and pushy, and give only a scant amount of detail about themselves or their dogs, and are much more focused on money. Their dogs may not be in the best of condition or health – a Whippet will show it is unhappy both in its mannerisms and its eyes. Never buy an unseen puppy from the back of a car at a rendezvous. Money is the only reason that these people breed puppies, and they have scant regard for their dogs. You should never buy from such people.

For this reason, it is vital that you visit the breeder and see what Whippets they have and the puppies they have available. Ask about the other puppies, especially if you are only offered one from the litter. Get to know the breeder, and don't be afraid to ask any questions. They should be able to show you the mother (also known as the dam) of the puppies, as well as the whole litter together. Sometimes they have the father (known as the sire) of the puppies also, though this may not often be the case as breeders use other breeders' dogs at stud – but they at least should have a photo of him for you to see. They probably will have more than one generation at home. You should also ask what health testing the parents have had, and the results of those tests. Most health-testing schemes issue a certificate that shows the results of that testing; currently eye tests and heart tests are the ones you should ask about.

The puppies may not be old enough to leave the breeder on your first visit. You would probably be able to visit for a viewing when the puppies are around six weeks old, and if this is not possible, a lot of preparation and discussion of the kind outlined above should have taken place. But if you are making a first visit around that time, they should be weaned from their mother and eating well, and the breeder should have wormed the puppies by this age. In general, the puppies should be outgoing, fairly quiet (as in not noisy) and settled, playing happily together.

Sometimes you find your soul mate immediately.

None of the puppies should be lethargic or subdued, they should have clear eyes free from discharge, and their coat should be shiny and sleek.

If the puppies are listless, potbellied, and their gums and tongue are pale and not bright pink, they may be full of worms. Beware of any discharge from their eyes and/or nose – it may be a sign that they may be suffering from a disease such as parvovirus, which can be fatal. *Do not* buy a puppy like this, especially because you feel sorry for it – it may survive for only a few weeks and you will have lost your money, have a hefty vet's bill, and no puppy at the end of it.

All the breeder's dogs should be in good health; if there are a large number of dogs and of different breeds, or they bring out just one puppy for you to see without letting you see the remainder of the litter, it is possible that they may not be reputable breeders and you should not buy from them. It is important that you do not feel under pressure to buy; if you are at all uncertain that the puppies are not for you, walk away. Never make a purchase

The puppies may not be ready to leave home yet but should be adventurous and full of character.

because you feel sorry for the puppies. However, if you feel comfortable that this is the right breeder and you are happy with the puppies and their 'family', you can begin to choose your new puppy!

The breeder should be happy to guide you in deciding on which puppy would be suitable for you. For example, if you are simply wanting a pet, there may be some of the litter that are not going to 'make the grade' for the breeder and they would be happy for them to go with that in mind. You must be honest with the breeder as to what your intention is, because if, for example, the puppies are from show parents and you decide later to show your pet, the breeder might have suggested a different puppy with that in mind. Remember, when you take on your puppy, you are also representing that breeder and they only want the best specimens to be shown. The breeder will be on hand to advise you about the correct way to train your puppy to fulfil its potential.

One of the other responsible duties of a breeder is that they should supply a 'puppy pack'.

Puppy Pack

A puppy pack can be in different formats but basically first of all should include The Kennel Club registration certificate, if the puppies are advertised as 'KC Reg. puppies'. There may also be a contract, which

Choosing your new puppy can be difficult – in a good litter all the puppies look the same!

Puppies go through different stages – even their ears change!

may include any restrictions or conditions of sale. It is important that you read this carefully, and make sure you understand and are happy with the content before signing it. Sometimes a breeder will impose restrictions, such as the puppy cannot be bred from and should be neutered. This is usually because they feel the puppy is not of good enough quality for breeding or show. Alternatively there may be a situation where the breeder would like to have puppies back from your puppy at some time in the future, either as a stud dog or a breeding bitch.

This must be extremely carefully thought out and discussed before you make a purchase and sign the agreement. If you are inexperienced and have never bred a litter before, and are not used to having a stud dog, it is a big undertaking to commit to this. The breeder may reduce the price of the puppy to facilitate this agreement, which at the time seems appealing, but it is a long-term commitment you are making with the breeder. It is much more advisable to pay the full purchase price, especially if you have any doubts whatsoever, and the puppy is then yours outright.

The following information should be provided:

- A diet sheet that sets out what kind of food your puppy has been reared on and is used to eating, and how many times a day it is fed.

- The dates your puppy has been wormed for roundworm, and an outline of the ongoing worming programme.
- A health check confirmation, which should have been carried out by the breeder's vet.
- A vaccination certificate that gives details of the puppy's treatment.
- And most importantly, the unique microchip number of your puppy. The law requires the breeder to microchip the puppy by the time it is eight weeks old. This will be transferred into your name when you purchase the puppy, and this should be included in the puppy price. Confirmation of transfer into your ownership will follow shortly after purchase from the microchip database.

If your puppy is Kennel Club registered you will be given a certificate of registration, which will show all the puppy's details – the breeder should sign the transfer portion. To transfer the puppy into your name you should complete the back of the form and either send it with the required fee to The Kennel Club registration department, or this can be done online using your puppy's unique code, which is also on the certificate. As mentioned in the next chapter, a comfort blanket is useful, and the breeder will probably provide a small amount of food that you can take home with you.

Leaving his siblings is a big step for this brindle puppy.

Keep in Touch

This is the beginning of an exciting and rewarding time, and many breeders like to keep in touch and hear about the milestones of your puppy's life. If they are a dedicated breeder, it is interesting for them to see your pet in later life, and see how they have developed and grown into your pride and joy. A good breeder never shirks their responsibility to the puppies they have bred and should in most cases discuss with you the situation where, if for any reason you are unable to keep your Whippet, it should be returned to them as the breeder. This may form part of your contract, as many breeders would prefer to have a puppy returned, either to stay with them or to find it another suitable home.

Probably the best advice is to do your homework, and listen to the recommendations of others who have had a puppy from a breeder – but most of all, be sure that you are comfortable about having a Whippet for life.

Even a fly needs investigating.

CHAPTER 4

Health and Welfare

Bringing Your Puppy Home

If you have decided to have a puppy from a litter, it is a good idea to give the breeder a small blanket to put in with the puppies for a day or two, so that when you take your puppy home, it has a familiar-smelling item to comfort it and make it feel more secure in its new environment. It is a very big change for such a small person: everything is changing and it is suddenly on its own.

Today's the day! You are collecting your puppy from the breeder. After all the formalities, you are leaving with your puppy. It is comforting for the puppy if on this occasion, you travel with it on your knee; this gives it reassurance and can help to prevent travel sickness. Even so, it may be car sick or dribble saliva, so it is a good idea to have a towel to hand, and a plastic carrier bag packed with paper towels so any sickness can be caught quite easily. The alternative is to put your puppy in a travelling crate with a good selection of blankets and/or towels or a puppy pad. It may cry for a while as you set off, but will eventually fall asleep. It is easy to clean up a crate, and using it is a good start if you intend to use a crate when travelling in the future.

On arrival at home, your puppy will appreciate a run in the garden, not only to clean itself but to get a breath of fresh air, especially if it has been travel sick. The breeder may have given the puppies a light meal a few hours before leaving, so after your puppy has had a run around, offer it a small drink of milk or water. This replaces some fluids and prepares its stomach for a solid meal. Your puppy will probably love to run around and explore for a while. You can then offer it one of its main meals, and allow it to continue exploring its new surroundings. You should

Everything is very strange to begin with, but your puppy will soon find its feet.

offer a lot of cuddles to reassure your new puppy that it is not alone and vulnerable.

Toilet Training

When you bring your puppy home it is probable that it has already begun its house training, or at least will be trained to a newspaper or puppy pad. This should be placed near the outside door so the puppy begins to establish what that exit means. It will soon go instinctively to the pad. If it does not, and soils on the floor elsewhere, carry it to the pad whilst giving a command. Another way is to take it outside as soon as it wakes up, after it has

Lots of cuddles create a bond: a puppy loves being with you.

eaten or drunk, and periodically in between. Give your command, and when it 'performs', praise it. This can be repeated every time, and soon by taking the puppy outside into your garden, it will know what is expected of it.

Although it may be quicker to lift the puppy up and take it outside, by encouraging it to walk out with you, it will associate this route and destination with cleaning itself. This should be repeated every time – it may seem tedious at first, but it is well worth sticking to it, and certainly much better than having your Whippet soiling in the house. It is also useful to associate a word with toilet training, so that when you are away from home, the puppy understands it is acceptable to perform on a strange area.

You should not take your puppy out anywhere in public until it has been fully vaccinated.

Visit to the Vet

Once your puppy has settled into its new home, you should make an appointment with your local vet. This is a way of introducing your puppy to the vet as well as checking that it is well and making good progress. You may need to complete its vaccination sequence, and your vet will advise on worming – they will probably ask for previous worming dates so they can establish a programme. Also, if you haven't needed to have a vet before,

you are making a contact just in case they are needed; many vets run a health plan, which is a good way of keeping your pet healthy through regular dental and general health checks.

Puppy Food

One of the most important times for a Whippet is when it is growing, and it is vital that it has the best puppy food you can afford, at least while it is growing and developing. Your breeder will have outlined on the diet sheet which puppy food they have been using, and how many feeds they have been giving the puppies each day, and probably would give you some of the same food to take home. During the short time of its puppyhood when it is growing so fast, it is extremely important to provide the puppy with a correctly balanced food. This is essential for providing the necessary vitamins and minerals, as well as the right protein percentage to ensure strong bones and a healthy constitution, at the right growth rate.

To avoid your puppy developing an upset tummy it is best to keep to the brand your breeder recommends. If you wish to change to another kind, introduce the new food in small amounts over several days until the changeover is complete. If you do want to change the food, it is best to seek advice about a similar puppy food to ensure good growth and development. Many pet-food firms have excellent products on the market, suited to the size and breed of dog. Pet stores have properly trained consultants who can advise you on the correct choice if you are unsure.

Time For Bed

Equally as important as food is rest. Your puppy will sleep quite a lot at first and it is important that he should be allowed to sleep undisturbed, as this is vital to ensure correct development. If you have children in the family or as visitors, it is important that they allow the puppy to sleep when it wants to. For this reason, a dog crate or cage is very useful. These are widely available from most pet stores in a variety of sizes and colours. Make sure you buy a crate that will still be the right size when your puppy is an adult, probably one that allows it enough room to stand up and move around comfortably.

A cosy bed, snuggling under the covers: Whippet heaven.

The puppy will soon regard the crate as its safe haven and will retire into it to sleep or to go for a quiet time with its toys. It is also useful to put the puppy into if you go out, or for security in the back of the car when travelling. Most Whippets are happy to use these cages as their bed – they can be put into the cage at night. This ensures they are safe, and if you are still house training, prevents accidents in the house. There may be a few whines or sing songs from your puppy to start with, but it will soon settle into its routine and know that 'that means bedtime'. Your Whippet should not be left for long periods in the cage, but if it feels it is a secure place, it will often retire there on its own. It is best to leave the door open when you are at home, so the puppy can go in and out as it pleases, and doesn't feel it is a 'sin bin'.

Alternatively you may wish to buy a standalone soft bed. These beds come in many varieties of shape, colour and materials. It is worth mentioning that when puppies are small they do like to chew, and it would be advisable to buy a modestly priced bed to start with. They take great delight in chewing and 'digging', and once they make a hole in the fabric, find that it's tremendous fun to pull the stuffing out of them. When they have grown up, a more luxurious bed would be appreciated, and they are more likely to chew their toys than the bed – but not always!

Basic Training For Your Whippet

It is essential to establish an 'understanding' with your new Whippet puppy. It will have a strong determination, and it is vital you establish some ground rules from the very beginning. As your puppy grows it will become more inquisitive and outgoing, it will be lively and boisterous, and its small milk teeth are very sharp. A puppy will chew anything, so it is important to remove or at least guard against any items that could be dangerous or that you treasure. It may seem like fun that the puppy chews your slippers, but it doesn't know the difference between those and your designer shoes.

Dog treats are an ideal way to train your puppy, to reward it when it reacts to your commands. They are an important aid. Always start with a simple task such as 'sit'. Hold your puppy's collar and gently but firmly press down on its rump, at the same time saying 'sit' in a firm, decisive voice. After repeating this a few times each day, your puppy will soon know what to do and will sit on its own – particularly in anticipation of a treat. This can be expanded to other commands as each is mastered. It is important to be firm and to use a strong command, though never be unkind.

A Whippet is intelligent and will learn quickly, being eager to please. There is an instructive piece on training in Chapter 10. However, if you teach your Whippet to

Start some basic training as soon as you can. Your puppy will quickly learn to sit.

'speak' on command, be prepared for a lot of backchat! This may be amusing at first, but can lead to an annoying, persistent bark if not taught correctly. Whippets do have another vocalisation, which is a quiet, much nicer mumble. This is far preferable to a constant, demanding bark.

You may wish to establish that certain areas of the house are 'out of bounds' – this is quite acceptable and your Whippet will soon learn this, but it will need determined insistence on your part. A baby gate is a good way to keep your puppy out of these areas within the house until it gets used to its new home and is fully house trained. You will find that your puppy will very soon begin to learn basic obedience and respond to training, as Whippets have a very sharp mind and are eager to learn.

Your puppy can start to wear a soft collar when it is quite young. To start with, the collar will feel very itchy to the puppy and there will be a lot of scratching, but it will soon settle down and accept the collar. It is a legal requirement that your puppy wears a collar and lead when out and about, but this should be of a much more robust type. Whippet collars are broad to the front of the neck, this extra width being to prevent the whippet choking as it pushes forwards into its collar when out walking. There are many lovely collars available.

The collar should carry a tag giving your contact details, and information to show that your puppy is microchipped. This is vitally important for your puppy's safe return in the event of its getting lost, for whatever reason. It is essential that the collar fits well: it should be tight enough not to slip over the puppy's head, but with enough room under the collar for comfort. There is more information on choosing a collar and lead in Chapter 5.

More Puppy Food and Worms

As your puppy grows it is important to make sure the quantity of its food is still appropriate for it. The feeding guide given by manufacturers is exactly that: a guide. You may find that your puppy still seems to be hungry after the measured amount is eaten. One way of knowing if your puppy is getting enough food is that its ribs should be well rounded and covered – that is, you cannot see the ribs themselves. There should be plenty of weight over its back, especially over the hip bones – you should be able to feel these bones, but they should not be prominent, and certainly not sticking up. The speed at which a puppy actually eats is variable – you may have a slow, more sedate eater, or one that gulps down its food. In fact it is unwise to allow your Whippet to gulp down its food, and there are specialist feeding dishes available that slow down the rate of consumption. This prevents the puppy choking, and the risk of bloat in its stomach.

There is no point in buying a good quality food if you are feeding worms inside the puppy's stomach. If your puppy starts to lose a little weight and becomes 'ribby', if its stomach is big and rounded and feels very firm, it would be a good idea to worm it. You may see an occasional worm in its faeces that would indicate their presence, but this is not always the case. Good quality worming products can be bought over the counter or are available from your vet. It is also beneficial to change to a different brand occasionally, so the worms don't become resistant; your vet may have packages available that include regular health checks, which should include

Robust, safe toys are ideal. Cheaper ones are quickly demolished.

Spending time with your puppy develops its personality.

a worming programme. Your breeder will have told you the date when the puppy was last wormed.

Regular worming is strongly advisable throughout the dog's life. *Toxicara canis* (roundworm) can be a health hazard if faeces are not picked up, as they can be transferred to humans.

Healthy Puppies

A Whippet puppy is normally very healthy and robust. It should have bright eyes and a cold nose, and be energetic and lively. It is possible that your new puppy has a mildly upset stomach for a day or so after its arrival: this can be a combination of the stress of travelling and settling into a new home, but if it continues on the same regime as followed by its breeder, this should soon settle down. However, if your puppy begins to refuse food and, more importantly, refuses to drink, and if it becomes listless and has a temperature (a dry, hot nose is an indicator) and watery diarrhoea, you must call the vet immediately, as its condition may be serious.

On a day-to-day basis your puppy should be eating and drinking normally, and it is important that fresh water is always available. Do not allow it to drink any water or liquid that may contain harmful chemicals. The toilet pan is a special favourite, and anti-freeze is very poisonous – unfortunately it tastes sweet, which might make it appealing to your puppy. Many of our foods, substances and plant materials are harmful to a puppy, and it is useful to familiarise yourself with these. Prevention is much better than cure or death.

Exercise

Exercise is as important to your puppy as good food and sleep. Once your puppy has been fully vaccinated and is used to its collar, you can start taking it for short walks on the lead out of your garden. This should be at a leisurely pace, as your puppy will be much more interested in exploring its surroundings than walking too far – so short, leisurely walks to begin with, then gradually increasing the length of time spent out as the puppy gets stronger. The walks should never be too long, nor at too fast a pace, as your puppy's legs are still very supple and over-exercise can cause damage to its growing bones.

The best exercise is allowing your puppy to run freely around the garden so it can stop when it feels tired. You can play with it, or maybe start some short spells of training to stimulate it, but again you should not force the pace. This is a much more 'natural' approach to exercise, and beneficial in that it strengthens the bones and muscles correctly. Your puppy shouldn't be allowed to stand on its hind legs for any length of time, nor to jump up to any height, as this also puts a strain on growing legs.

It is also important that your puppy doesn't pull on the lead: there is no worse sight than an owner being dragged around by their dog. Whippets do push into their collars naturally, but this should not be a strong pull, where you are fighting against the pull. Encourage the puppy to walk alongside you or 'to heel' on a loose lead; it can be a good idea to interject the walk with a few sits, when a treat is offered. This is also good to use when at the kerbside, so your puppy learns to sit before crossing the road. Do not allow your puppy to bark and chase anything when out on the lead: reprimand it with a strong '*no*' and move away from the problem as if you are frightened of it – this is always a good way to teach a puppy about livestock.

As your puppy gets bigger you may allow it to gallop for short spells – this helps to build up and tone muscles, and to work the heart and lungs. If you do not have a large area for this type of exercise at home, it is important that you use a dedicated dog exercise field or a secure area. Always stay aware of your surroundings, and anything that may attract your puppy's unwanted attention: if your puppy is distracted it may not come back to you. You should always try to be one step ahead at recognising a potential hazard. However, this is a joyful time for your puppy as all Whippets love to run, and for you there is no better sight than seeing it in a full flowing gallop.

Training Clubs

Once your puppy has passed the babyhood stage and becomes a much more established youngster, you will begin to see a young adult appearing. Your basic training and rearing can now move on to thinking about more formal training, or extending their repertoire. There are many good training clubs that offer a warm welcome, with specialised coaching for both owner and Whippet in any sport you wish to take part in. There is no pressure to do intense training: it is all at your own pace, and experts will advise you accordingly as to the best way

A favourite is free running – great fun and natural exercise.

forwards, and can quickly assess the qualities of your Whippet.

The important thing is that it is fun for both you and your Whippet, and this will probably mould its development – and the end result is a well-trained, polite youngster with a sense of fun and probably competitiveness! It is great to have such a hobby together with your Whippet, and often the children in a family take on these sports and do exceptionally well. A Whippet is also a good teacher for children, who will learn about the responsibilities of looking after a pet; it will also provide them with a great hobby or sport, which many youngsters will embrace with great enthusiasm. There is more about this in Chapter 10.

CHAPTER **5**

Temperament

By nature the Whippet has a personality that few can resist. They are as happy charging around at high speed as they are snuggled down fast asleep. Many years ago, not having owned a Whippet, I always thought the Whippet was a small, shivery, pathetic dog. They often looked unhappy, ears down, tail between their legs, and disinterested in the showing environment especially. I was not alone, and have heard several other people's accounts over the years, people who viewed the breed similarly and came to the same conclusions. Little did I know then, that for over fifty years Whippets would be the centre of my world, as they are for those other sceptics who are now also established Whippet owners! But beware, one is never enough! They have an irresistible charm.

The Whippet is never happier than running free, but they also love being competitive. Racing around is their passion, and they get quite irate if they are not included in the 'race'. I remember one owner who left her Whippet in the car while she went to run another dog at a race meeting, and returned to find only the remains of a well chewed steering wheel! Such is their level of frustration, competitiveness and determination.

Your Whippet can be a joy to own, and a much treasured, intelligent family member; this may suit your lifestyle, and it will be perfectly happy and content. They are easily trained and sensitive to your emotions; many are trained as PAT dogs and companions to disabled owners. They will be as active as you wish, and are not demanding, but they do appreciate a routine to their life. Our expectations haven't changed for over a hundred years, although we are not expecting our pet to provide the weekly meat

Whippets are very loving and close companions.

ration! The Whippet's handy size and adaptability lends itself to being the ideal companion. So, what happened to that small, shivery thing? Rest assured, they can play that card when necessary: bring on a cold wind, the slightest suggestion of inclement weather or – horrors! – when the nail clippers come out! But on a good day there is no finer sight than a proud Whippet striding out on the lead.

All hound breeds have an inbuilt instinct to hunt or chase, and the Whippet is no exception. You should be aware that the sporting side is still very much a part of their character. That energy can be channelled into taking part in some sporting discipline such as racing, lure coursing and obedience, and such sports as agility and fly ball. They will enjoy these activities with great enthusiasm, and it doesn't matter at what age you decide to begin in a sport, they will be open to learning a new skill.

This instinct to chase includes cats, although if you have a cat already at home, when your Whippet puppy arrives, the cat will most probably establish who is in charge: a few pats with their clawed foot is usually enough to earn respect from your puppy. A cat's natural instinct is to run when threatened, which is exactly what your Whippet wants, but if this understanding is achieved early on, your cat will probably stand its ground, and this is no fun whatsoever to your Whippet.

A cautionary point here: always be in full control of your Whippet when out walking, whether in the town or in the countryside, because for the Whippet, the temptation to chase is very strong, and anything that runs is of interest. The Whippet, being a sighthound, will be alerted to any sudden movement in the grass, or livestock in a field, and will not heed your commands once its attention is focused elsewhere. Always keep it on a lead, well under control, and if you have to pass through such areas be prepared for the unexpected! Even on the lead they can pull quite strongly if alerted. Several owners have been pulled over by their sudden strength on the lead, especially if they are out with a few Whippets, and it is very easy to get the lead wrapped around your legs.

It is instinctive for a Whippet to investigate anything that moves in the undergrowth.

A Whippet collar is broad in design and can be made of leather or pretty patterned webbing.

Collars and Leads

Whippet collars are specially designed for Whippets, with a broad front and strong buckle; the best are made of leather, although alternative synthetic types are cheaper. The lead should be of sturdy leather with a loop handle and a strong catch to fix to the collar. It is better to have a lead with stitching rather than a rivet. A rivet can give way without warning, but a stitched leather lead gives you some indication of the wear and tear it has suffered. Always choose a fairly long lead that allows your Whippet to walk on ahead without you tripping over it. It is much easier that way if you are exercising more than one at a time.

It is also important to have a close-fitting collar. It should be buckled up to be a neat fit so the collar can't slip over the ears, but not too tight – you should be able to fit two fingers comfortably between the Whippet's neck and the collar when it is fitted.

Laying Down A Few Ground Rules

Having a puppy is time-consuming, and it is important to lay down a few ground rules through discipline and training, as discussed later in the book. The foundation for your future life with your Whippet will depend on how you navigate these first few months. Puppies are so appealing and it is hard to be strict with them, but strict you must be. A Whippet's determination to get its own way will test you sometimes to your limits, but you must be even more determined to succeed than your puppy is. Just one lapse on your part will change the lights to green for your puppy.

You will see its character develop as it grows, and by the time it is nearing twelve months old and is no longer the cute little puppy, you will see a much more streetwise dog emerge. As with any 'teenager', it will have its moments and will try to rebel occasionally, but you will begin to see a young adult develop in character and a devoted companion unfurl. This period in your puppy's life can be a time of exploration, but also insecurity – sighthounds are by nature quite reserved, and despite all the bravado, there will be times when they need some reassurance. Whippets are generally willing to bark if a stranger is encroaching on their territory, but will quickly stop if reassured, although a few rumbles in the throat might still continue! Sometimes the most mundane things can alarm them – for instance, a plastic bin bag put out for collection, rattling in the wind.

The best approach is to settle your Whippet by reassuring it, then approach the 'noise' and let it sniff it, so it can see that it is not threatening. This sort of thing can sometimes take a few tries, but if your bond is strong enough, the puppy will rely on you to show it what to do, and eventually will decide for itself that it is nothing more than rubbish.

Loved by all the family, especially children.

Having More Than One Whippet

Males are quite loyal and devoted to their owners, and generally make more loving pets, and under normal circumstances will get on well together. As adults, Whippets can be quite independent in their manner, and this characteristic is usually found to be stronger in females. If you are thinking of having more than one whippet, you should bear in mind that if they do not arrive together, the resident Whippet may resent the new addition to the family. If this is the case, the best way to deal with it is to bring your resident Whippet out for a walk and allow them to meet in a neutral place. They should soon settle down to live happily together.

A word of caution: if you are having two bitches, they will get along very well most of the time, but as they approach the time when they come into season, they can get very hormonal and can become unsettled (of course this doesn't happen if they have been neutered). Often the more dominant of the two will try and pick a fight. Your other bitch may be submissive and they will settle back down, but if she decides to stand her ground, they may start to physically fight one another. This sounds, and is, frantic, and it is important that as the 'boss', you stop this as they will quite quickly cause injury to one another.

If they have been well trained and interact with you, a strong word from you should be sufficient to stop the affray in its tracks, but if they continue it may be necessary to intervene. Here you should be extremely careful

A Whippet is not demanding and loves home comforts...

...but always keeps an eye on what's going on.

that you don't get bitten in the confusion. *Never* put your hand down to try and separate them. A rolled-up newspaper will make a noise and distract them without harming them. At the same time you should use a firm voice to bring them under control, and part them. Allow them to 'cool off' in different rooms, then introduce them back together but under supervision, asserting your authority until they back down.

Once they have had an incident like this, they may do it again. To prevent the trouble flaring up again, watch out for the typical signs of aggression: raised hackles on the back of the neck, stiff leg movements, and a tail lifted higher than normal as one sets itself up to the other. The main thing is to pre-empt this fight reoccurring: using your firm voice should be enough to avert them. They will eventually understand that just lifting the newspaper is a signal to stop: hitting the newspaper on your hand makes a sharp noise, and along with your voice, should persuade them to settle back down.

A BAD TEMPERAMENT

Fortunately, a Whippet with a bad temperament is a rare occurrence. This is usually hereditary, passed down even from just one parent. In a puppy it is manifested as nervousness and not being outgoing, and when the puppy is put into a situation where they feel threatened or vulnerable, they will panic and bite. In puppyhood there is no excuse for this type of behaviour, and it is probable the puppy will grow to be a troublesome adult that can't be trusted. It could be that with an intense effort on your part to build trust with the puppy, they may come round and rely on you for support, but they will never be an outgoing Whippet. As an adult, a Whippet with a bad temperament is a liability that can't be trusted in and around people, and as a result they often lead a stressful and miserable life.

So you can see how important it is to lay the foundation of good training right from the beginning. This should be seen as a partnership, but a partnership in which you ultimately have the upper hand. A Whippet is very receptive to your body language, and will sense your mood and will offer comfort if it thinks you need it. There are times when it will forget itself and be mischievous out of frustration or just sheer fun. But it will take guidance from you, and often a knowing glance is sufficient.

As your Whippet gets older, its priorities will change, and the liveliest puppy will settle down into a calmer adult (most of the time!). Certainly there will always be a compulsion to race around, and a Whippet will never forget its natural instincts – but as your Whippet becomes an adult and leaves its sometimes challenging adolescent stage behind, a gentle and affectionate companion emerges. Whippets are not demanding and are happy to fit in with your plans, and even happier to have a duvet day!

CHAPTER **6**

Caring for the Adult Whippet

Adulthood can be said to be from the age of two years onwards: this is when your Whippet begins to look in their prime. You have lived through a cute, cuddly puppy, through adolescence when life is a great adventure, to enjoying your Whippet in adulthood as an elegant, curvy, devoted companion admired by many. The joys of owning a Whippet are both satisfying and comforting. Day to day, as with any family member, they like to have a structured routine and will happily settle into this. It is generally accepted that Whippets have a robust constitution, and with the right upbringing they will live to around fourteen years old – and it has been known for some to reach twenty years old! So, you can do your part in managing this expectation.

Day-To-Day Care

Food
Maintaining general health not only comes from regular exercise but also a balanced diet and a daily routine. A Whippet loves to eat and will over-indulge if given the chance; as already mentioned the feeding guide on the bag of food is just that: not all dogs have the same metabolism nor take the same amount of exercise, so you should use your own judgement. An overweight Whippet doesn't look good, nor will it want to exercise as it should, and it will easily slip into being a couch potato. This excess weight begins to put a strain on the body.

Complete foods are easy to use and measure, so regulating their weight should be quite easy. A Whippet should never look bony and thin nor very round and fat,

It's easier to manage portions if the dogs eat from their own bowls.

but healthy and shapely. Because of their love for food, using treats as a training aid is very easy, but these should be kept to a minimum at all other times. Not only does it keep an interest in the treat and therefore the training, but it helps to keep that slim, healthy look. Complete foods don't require any additions, and Whippets love to hear themselves crunching. It depends on your budget: there are complete foods available at a range of prices. You may find that some foods do not agree with your Whippet and cause diarrhoea, and finding what suits them best is a case of trial and error.

A Raw Diet

A raw diet is very popular nowadays, harking back to more traditional feeding regimes. If you wish you can add beef, green tripe (not bleached as in the butcher's shop), raw or cooked chicken or fish, perhaps occasionally raw chicken wings. Beef and tripe are both available minced or in chunks, and are freely available from good pet stores in frozen packs. This makes it more interesting for your Whippet, and they usually relish eating such foods. It is essential that cooked chicken is boned before feeding to your Whippet as the cooked bones become very sharp and can get stuck in their throat.

Raw vegetables and fruit such as carrots and apples are also 'fun' food. You can introduce all kinds of extras, but make sure you are aware that some foods that we enjoy are toxic to dogs. Fresh water should be available at all times.

Exercise

As pointed out earlier, you must be well aware of the Whippet's inherent natural instincts. The Whippet was bred to chase and catch rabbit or hare, and despite your Whippet being a much loved family member, it can quickly revert

The Risk of Bloat

In the health issues section, bloat is mentioned. Very few Whippets have been affected by this problem, but to prevent it from occurring it is essential that your Whippet eats more than one meal a day. As humans, we usually eat two good meals a day with perhaps a snack for lunch to satisfy our hunger, and your Whippet, even in adulthood, should have at least two meals a day. This doesn't mean you need to increase their food ration, but you can split the daily amount in two. Keeping food in the stomach prevents the build-up of excessive gas, which can cause the stomach to twist, which is bloat. This is an urgent, life-threatening problem: if your Whippet is looking unwell and becomes very quiet and their stomach area is distended and hard to touch, they need urgent veterinary attention.

Raw meat and bones are natural food, and make meal times more interesting.

Agile jumping and twisting – a natural way to play.

to that inherited behaviour if the chance arises. Out in the countryside, it is wise always to have your Whippet on a lead, not only if you are near farming livestock, but also should a wild animal emerge out of the undergrowth unexpectedly. You may not believe it, but a pet is capable of bringing down a wild animal much larger than itself, and Whippets have been known to catch deer.

Do not walk in a field where there are cows with calves at foot. The cow will protect her calf, and all too often there have been cases of walkers with their dogs that have been trampled, suffering serious injury or death. If you let your Whippet off the lead anywhere, make sure that not only are there no livestock in close proximity, but also that the area is secure. Once your Whippet is loose, you have lost a certain degree of control, and if, for instance, a rabbit or squirrel pops up, they will give chase and 'go deaf' to even your most earnest calling. Always be alert to your surroundings, just as much as your Whippet is.

As your Whippet grows it will get increasingly strong as its bones develop and muscle builds, all due to correct exercise. It is normal for a Whippet to revel in its ability to gallop, and this will build up a physique that enhances their curvaceous outline. This can easily be maintained by a mix of walking on the lead, galloping freely, and natural play at home in the garden. The Whippet is renowned for enjoying a 'mad half-hour', which involves them charging around, at high speed, round and round for no apparent reason. This exercises and tones up their heart, lungs and muscles. At this age, once developed, their physique can easily be maintained. As your Whippet gets older and slower its muscle tone will decrease slightly and become softer – however, occasional bursts of energy show that it is still in its mind to 'have a go'. At any age your Whippet will enjoy being out with you.

Grooming

One of the most pleasurable tasks associated with Whippet care is grooming. The Whippet has a fine, short coat that is easily kept clean and requires a minimum of care compared to breeds with a heavier coat. They do moult some hair during the year, but this is easily removed with regular brushing with a soft-bristled brush or a rubber hound glove – this fits over the hand as a glove, and has a soft bristle or soft rubber side that is good for removing dead hair. A Whippet loves this type of grooming as it also acts as a type of massage.

Sometimes that itch just needs a nibble!

Whippets are always keen to find something extremely smelly or decomposed while out walking, and then rubbing and rolling themselves in it, and a bath or shower is occasionally necessary! You should use a dog shampoo as these productions are specifically developed to maintain the correct balance of natural oils in the coat. Gently warmed water and a good rub all over will remove the dirt quite easily and rinse off the shampoo completely – and then be prepared for a good shake! A good rub with a clean towel removes excess water, and they can be dried either naturally or on a gently warm setting on a hair drier. Naturally they dry fairly quickly in a warm room, and with a good brush to smooth the coat, are soon back to normal, smelling sweetly with a glistening coat.

During the winter months, make sure they are not allowed to get chilled after a bath as they will not be fully dry down to the skin for a few hours. The Whippet's coat is fine textured and doesn't grow a thick undercoat so it is good to have a fitted Whippet coat for them for the winter months or inclement days while out exercising. They come in a variety of styles and materials: thick, warm and weatherproof is ideal. They do so love to show off!

Ears

Generally caring for the Whippet's ears is relatively simple. Check periodically that they are clean – Whippets don't normally have ear troubles. There are various ear cleaners available from pet stores in the form of wipes, liquid or powder. Do not be tempted to delve deep into their ears with a cotton bud or other item, remove any dirt or wax from the outer ear with a wipe or a piece of damp cotton wool. If their ears become smelly and

Whippet coats come in many designs and fabrics.

Persistent ear scratching should be checked out.

they start to shake their head or try to scratch at their ear repeatedly, seek veterinary advice. They may have developed canker in the ear and this needs attention.

During the summer months it is advisable to take care of the outer flap of the ears as they can be subject to sunburn. This part of the ear is very fine and delicate, with only a fine covering of hair. A small drop of suncream can protect them. In winter they may be subject to frostbite if outside for too long – this is always worth checking. The outer ear flap is a good indicator as to whether they are feeling the cold. There are some fabulous snoods available that give both warmth and protection.

Teeth

Teeth can be cleaned, but often dry biscuits and occasional chews can remove a lot of dirt. It is soft food that encourages teeth to become dirty, and after a while the build-up results in plaque on the teeth. Some pet groomers will clean the dog's teeth, or your vet would do this service, especially if there is tartar that has hardened and can be difficult to remove. However, it is easy enough to do it yourself from the word go, and this reduces any build-up on the teeth. There are dog toothpastes and plaque removers available, and a good medium-strength toothbrush should do the trick. Pay particular attention to the back molars, as often food gets stuck between these teeth and the inside of the cheek – it can be removed with your finger. The concentration of tartar over a period of time can lead to tooth decay, which can be painful and causes smelly breath, so it is good practice to keep up the cleaning regime, or at least have the teeth checked regularly.

Nail Trimming

Nail trimming is essential as a Whippet's nails grow incredibly fast and do need trimming back regularly. Most pet stores sell a range of nail clippers. This is a job that is best done from an early age, and the sooner the better. Not only does it allow your Whippet to get used to it and removes the possibility of a struggle, but

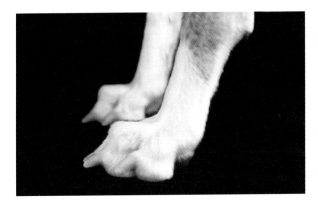

Nails should be the correct length and nicely shaped. The pink wick can be seen inside the nail.

it keeps the nails at a good length, minimising the risk of them scratching you or your furniture or wooden floors. Overgrown nails are unsightly, and if left, affect how your Whippet will walk; in some cases they could cause a toe injury, which will be uncomfortable. As a regular routine, the white tips of each nail can be trimmed back quite easily. It is easy to see the wick of the toes inside a white toenail, but more difficult if their nails are darker.

Trim the nail up to the end of the wick – and don't worry if you snip off a little too much and make it bleed. Hold the nail end with a little piece of damp cotton wool, and it will soon stop; products are also available to stop any bleeding. Dremmels are very popular for keeping nails short and lessen the risk of getting too near to the wick of the toe; they also can shape the nails nicely. It is advisable to start this regime right from beginning, when your Whippet is still a baby puppy. Many owners are not insistent enough, and this leads to a struggle and a battle of wills, and the owner gives up. However, if you insist and continue, the puppy will soon resign itself to being still and allowing you to trim the nails without much fuss.

A special note about winter walking on roads that have been treated with road salt: always wash your Whippet's feet with warm, clean water on returning home as the road salt may cause irritation to their feet.

Health Issues

It may be that even though your Whippet receives the best of care in its rearing, it has a health problem, or develops one. As discussed earlier, when buying your puppy, the breeder should have had a health check carried out by their vet, but some conditions do develop at a later date, or cannot be identified early in life. It is important that you don't panic, but ask your vet for advice initially, and they may well refer you to a vet who specialises in that field. Ask them if it is a common issue for the breed.

There are testing sessions for heart and eyes where you can take your Whippet: for a small fee you will be issued with a certificate outlining the findings, and given the results as a scoring. These results not only identify if there is a problem, but they are also graded as to their severity. This information is collated to give an overall view of the breed's health issues – it may identify a pattern, and point out if there is any cause for further investigation and research, as well as for your own information. This will be further discussed with you by the specialist.

Heart Murmurs

One example of a health issue that has been identified is that in some Whippet puppies, a heart murmur may be found in a routine vet check when they are five or six weeks old. Research is ongoing, but it has been found that in some cases, this murmur is evident during a certain stage of growth, but if the Whippet is retested as it gets older, the murmur has disappeared. If this is the case, it is wise to seek advice, but keep it in perspective. Whippets naturally have a condition called arrhythmia, which means that their heart normally beats more slowly than other breeds, but this increases when they gallop. This condition is peculiar to these types of running dog.

Anaesthetics and Bloat

Whippet owners should be sure to inform their vet should their Whippet require an anaesthetic: because Whippets are deep chested, sometimes they have a particular intolerance to some kinds of anaesthetic, which can cause problems, so it is best to mention this if the occasion arises. However, modern anaesthetics now are very good.

This is also the case with bloat. There are very few cases in Whippets, but it is known in other sighthounds. The stomach fills with gas and twists, causing excruciating pain and shock. The stomach is distended and hard to the touch, and the Whippet is obviously unwell. This is

A lovely group of Whippets.

an emergency and a life-threatening condition, so call your vet immediately.

If there is an unresolved health problem of any kind, ask your vet for advice from a specialist vet. This is a good reason for having pet insurance for your Whippet, as often health issues are expensive to treat.

The biggest health issue for Whippets, as concluded in a survey by pet insurers, is injury and trauma, which is not surprising considering the prevalence of a Whippet's 'mad half-hours'. The Whippet is known for its resilience to pain, and can be quite stoical even when suffering the most horrendous injuries, and will carry on regardless even after hurting itself. Unfortunately as a result, the injured Whippet's activities must be restricted to allow recovery – and often once the stage of 'feeling sorry for itself' has passed, the Whippet will be keen to return to normal. In this instance a crate is useful to restrict the Whippet's exercise when it is recuperating in order to help the healing process until the injury is mended and the Whippet is given the 'all clear' for normal exercise.

Veteran Care

A veteran is usually referred to as being over seven years old, but as far as a Whippet is concerned, at that age they are still spring chickens! Nothing is impossible, and they will pass this age and more with little or no change. Some are prone to greying around the face, but it is usually by the time they get to nine or ten years old that the biggest difference is seen. During exercise they will not have quite the same stamina for racing around for the same length of time as before, but they will still be eager to carry out their daily routine.

At this stage it is perhaps time to think about a specialist senior food that maintains mobility, as well as other supplements that will keep the Whippet's 'machine' well oiled. Care should be taken with nail trimming, and feet get a little sensitive, but it is still important that the older dog has a pedicure. Included in your vet's plan may be regular check-ups on teeth, which can start to deteriorate and may need attention. A painful tooth can make a Whippet feel miserable, and it may go off its food. A pointer to a bad tooth may be that its breath starts to smell bad.

A veteran of fifteen years, greying around the face.

In most cases with older Whippets it is business as usual, but just at a slower pace. As your Whippet gets into its teens it will undoubtedly lose muscle tone, and its sensory perception may alter. Deafness and blindness are both common in old age, but Whippets can be very adaptable in coping with this, and it may not become apparent to you straightaway. As they age, often their mobility gets rather shaky: they may need help to get up and down, but can still walk fairly well. They will still need to be clean and want to go outside, but incontinence is something that you may have to cope with. Your Whippet may be absolutely horrified that it has soiled inside, so don't make a big thing of it.

Mental health is important, and your veteran will want to keep to its usual routine. We all hope our Whippets will go on forever, but sadly this is not the case, and there may come a point when it is time to say goodbye. How much nicer it would be if they gently drifted away in their sleep, but when their quality of life is so reduced that they are unhappy, often the definitive decision will have to be made. Having spent their whole life with you, it is a hard decision, but only you know how they feel and what is best for them.

A healthy fourteen-year-old, still in charge.

These fifteen-year-old brothers are taking things a bit easier.

CHAPTER 7

Dog Showing and Judging

An Introduction to Showing

You may have seen dogs being shown at a local event, or perhaps you have watched the greatest dog show, Crufts, on television, and this has made you think about 'having a go' at showing. This can be anything from an occasional hobby where you attend just a few shows or unofficial events, to becoming more interested and showing every week all over the country. There are dog shows for everyone of all ages, and it is very exciting to be amongst people who share the love of Whippets.

Firstly, you can go along to many of your local events, such as agricultural shows where they have 'enter on the day' shows. These are called 'Companion Dog Shows' and are often advertised in conjunction with a fund-raising day or something similar. This is a fun day out and a good taster for showing. There are usually pedigree classes that are judged on a merit basis, followed by novelty classes such as 'Dog with the waggiest tail', 'Dog most like its owner', and so on. You will notice in the pedigree classes that the owners follow a set pattern of showing their dogs, and often these dogs are seasoned show dogs. You can learn a great deal by just watching these classes, and it will give you an insight into what serious dog showing is like.

If you think you would like to pursue this further, your Whippet must be Kennel Club registered, and the certificate must have you as the registered owner. There are show training classes around the country that specialise in showing, with experienced trainers who will help you along the way. It is not just your Whippet that will be trained, but you, as the handler, will also be trained in how to present your Whippet to the judge.

Many exhibitors started with their pet as a show dog, and although you may not become a top winner, it is a sociable way of spending time with your Whippet. You can do as much or as little as you choose, and to whatever level; however, this can be dependent on the show quality of your Whippet, how much time and effort you want to put into it, how much tread you have on your car tyres, and how deep your pocket is!

The Show Pose

If you are starting with a puppy or an older dog, you can add some show training into your daily routine. There are many photos in this book of show dogs standing in a show pose, to give you an idea. Begin to stand your

An eight-week-old puppy beginning to stand still on the table – even if only for a few seconds.

Whippet in a show pose on the ground, and when it is standing still for maybe fifteen to twenty seconds without moving, you could progress to it standing on a table. It is better to use a non-slip table, or a normal table with a non-slip mat. This acts as a great confidence booster for your Whippet as it feels more secure when it is on the table, and you are close enough to see how it looks, as well as being ready to catch it if it thinks of jumping off.

Gently place your Whippet's legs in the correct position and hold its head, and try to keep it there as long as possible – it may be only a few seconds! Repeat this a couple of times and your puppy will begin to stand for longer each session. This will all come with practice, but it is best started as early as possible.

Along with standing in position, you will also need to practise moving your Whippet in a straight line and at a pace that shows its movement. It is usual to have the Whippet on your left-hand side, and you can place the lead around its throat just behind its head. This gives you maximum control. Your Whippet may object to this to begin with, but if you give a gentle tug on the lead with a word of encouragement and maybe offer a treat, it should begin to move with you. Walk briskly in a straight line, then turn to come back, keeping your Whippet on your left. Go into a standing position. Repeat this for maybe ten to fifteen minutes each day, and very soon your Whippet will have mastered the basics.

Training Classes

As with any hobby, there is a cost involved in attending training classes, as you will be required to pay a small amount per session; they are usually held on weekday evenings in a local church hall or community centre.

When you attend these classes the basic thing you will need is a show lead. These come in many styles, colours and varieties, so ask your trainer what they would suggest before buying something that might be unsuitable. It may be possible that they can get one for you at an upcoming show. You don't need to buy a lot of equipment for your Whippet to begin with, and you can use the grooming brushes you already have, but it is advisable maybe to take your Whippet's crate along with you – then they can securely watch what is going on, as they sometimes find it all rather daunting to begin with. They may be seeing some peculiar four-legged fluff balls they've never seen before.

Often you will not be alone in attending for the first time – and equally there may be someone attending the classes who is experienced in Whippets and is willing to give you advice on how to show your dog in a more specific way – but usually the class trainers are very good instructors. The evening is generally run either as a class at a dog show, or as individual training with the instructor on a one-to-one basis. In the class scenario you will first be asked to 'stand' your dog. This means you are standing your dog so the judge can walk down the ring and see it in profile. Your Whippet should be standing with its legs in the correct position and its head facing forwards.

Next you will be asked to 'put your dog on the table'. This is something highlighted in the first paragraph, and you should practise at home – a small, sturdy table with a non-slip surface is ideal. Stand your Whippet, again in profile to the judge. This may take quite a bit of practice, and it is a much easier task if your Whippet has done this from an early age; as it gets older it may be apprehensive

A show pose: all feet facing forwards and head held high.

When your Whippet is confident about standing still on the table, a titbit can be offered.

A training class replicates a show class, and prepares both handler and Whippet to compete in the breed classes.

about being at such a height, and start to tremble, which in turn makes the table wobble! It may also fidget, but don't worry because even the best show dogs do this! Whatever happens when your Whippet is on the table, do *not* let it fall off as this can put it off completely.

The 'judge' will examine your Whippet's teeth, then run their hands over its head and body looking for various points. You should be in full control of your Whippet as this happens, because it might react in an unexpected way! The 'judge' will then ask to see your Whippet moving.

Gently lift your Whippet from the table on to the floor and readjust your lead. Take your time, and with a word of encouragement to your Whippet, start to walk down the mat in a straight line to the bottom, then return to the 'judge'. Your walking pace should be such that your Whippet can do a gentle trot. The 'judge' is assessing where your Whippet places its feet to see if it is moving correctly. Your instructor may advise you to change the speed or to do something different that is more advantageous to your dog. They may also instruct you, as the handler, to make you look more professional. An experienced judge at a show can usually tell if the handler knows what they are about.

The judge feels for the layback of the shoulder.

Having returned to your place, you are then required to stand your Whippet again while the 'judge' makes their choice. At a proper show that is the basic sequence of what happens in the ring. It takes much practice to perfect this performance, and you would be as well to do this for maybe fifteen minutes every day at home.

You will find a lot of camaraderie amongst those who attend the training classes, and they will support you. Any wins at shows by members will often have a celebration at the class, and after a show has taken place people will always be asking how you've done. It's encouraging to spot a friendly face at your first few shows, too. Being a beginner can be very daunting to start with, but everyone started somewhere, and dedicated practice will result in a partnership that you and your Whippet can enjoy.

Your next step is to go to a show. You may choose to continue attending the Companion Dog Shows to start with, in order to gain experience: these shows are the lowest level of showing – the next level is to enter for a local dog show. These are run by clubs and societies all over the country, and there are regular set dates when shows are held. Your training club will have schedules available of upcoming local shows, and they can help you to do your entry form. This must be completed and sent in by a closing date with the entry fees; some can be entered online. You will need the registration details of your Whippet to enter. There is often a Whippet class in the schedule as they are popular show dogs, so you could be competing in your first breed class!

Preparing for the Show

Once you have completed your entry, you will have retained or printed off the show schedule, which gives you all the details about the show: venue, judges, date and time of judging, and rules and regulations of the show. It is important that you read these, because by signing the entry form you are confirming that you will abide by the rules set out by The Kennel Club. Before the show you may wish to bath your Whippet, but for a small show it is not always necessary if it is clean. Its nails should be trimmed and its teeth clean.

The night before the show you can collect up your schedule, collar and lead, show lead, crate with a comfortable blanket, a dish for drinking water and some treats. There are usually catering facilities at the show but check in the schedule, or take a picnic for yourselves. The venue may be outside or in a hall, and either of these could get cold so take your Whippet's coat just in case, and be comfortably dressed yourself with sensible shoes. You will also need a clip or a secure pin to secure your exhibitor number card when in the ring; ask your training instructor to give you some help with this, as again, there are many types.

Show Day

Leave in plenty of time to arrive at the show – at the very least, half an hour before judging is scheduled to start. Find a place to set up your crate that is near to the ring where you will be showing; you can walk your Whippet around the show to allow it to adjust to the surroundings. Do not allow your Whippet to approach other dogs unless it is under correct control: exhibitors could become irate if your Whippet buries its nose in their exhibit's coat, which took hours of grooming and trimming. Keep an eye on the progress of judging, and be ready when your class is called.

You can buy a catalogue that lists all the dogs entered at the show: it will have your Whippet's details listed in the class(es) you have entered, along with all the other dogs entered in your class; you can also follow the order of judging with this. It is advisable to watch what is happening in the ring as it gives you an idea of what the judge is asking the exhibitors to do. Soon it will be time to go into the ring. You can begin to prepare for the class: allow your Whippet to go outside into the exercise area in case they want to clean themselves, and then put on their show lead and brush them to be ready when the class is called.

Even the most seasoned exhibitor gets nervous before showing, so don't worry, you're not alone. When your class is called, enter the ring and find a place in the line of dogs. On your first time it is advisable to stand in the middle or towards the end of the line of dogs – this gives you time to watch the exhibits before you and see how they show their dogs; it also helps you to know what the judge's instructions might be in your class. At the training class you may only have moved in a straight line, and this judge may ask all the dogs to move in a triangle, so watch what others do.

Remember always to keep your Whippet on the same side as the judge is standing: this allows them always to get a clear view. The judge has approximately two minutes to assess your Whippet, so thorough training means you can use this time to your Whippet's best advantage. Most judges will tolerate a slight amount of unruliness in a youngster, but it makes it harder for them to come to a positive decision about your dog if it is misbehaving. So good training is the key.

When your time comes to go to the table, all your training will come into effect. It is important to remain calm. The judge may ask how old your Whippet is, and when they have finished their assessment, they will ask

Keep your eyes on the judge at all times.

The judge is deciding on his winners.

to see your Whippet moving. They may ask you to do this again, or they will thank you, and you then return to the end of the line of 'seen' dogs. Once all the dogs have been seen by the judge, all dogs should be standing again in their line. The judge will then make their choice, placing the dogs first, second, third and reserve (fourth). The winning dogs move to the centre of the ring to collect their prize cards and the judge writes some comments down in their judge's book. If you are pulled out in the prize winners, congratulations!

Sadly, not all dogs can win, and many go home without a prize card; however, take the day as good experience – you will know what to expect next time. If this is you, don't be disheartened – maybe another judge will place your Whippet at another show, but if you don't win any prizes after a few tries maybe it would be sensible to ask someone's advice about whether your Whippet is worthy of winning prizes, or what you could do to improve, or if you would be better staying at home with your beloved pet and attend those fun shows instead.

Competition in Whippet classes is very high, and it can take quite a considerable time, and effort and money to become sufficiently experienced to show your Whippet to its best advantage and be successful. However, with practice and persistence it is achievable, and if your Whippet is of good enough merit, as the saying goes 'every dog has his day'. Many Whippet exhibitors at the highest level have shown their dogs for many years before they achieve their goal. You can set your sights to whatever you feel is achievable, as the show system caters for all levels.

If after a while you would like to show more frequently, there are Whippet clubs in most areas of the country. They all hold shows of different levels during the year, and such a show is a good place to go and watch, as well as being a good opportunity to meet other Whippet owners. You may like to become a member of the club – you will then receive newsletters and information of upcoming

The final line-up of winners is called into the centre of the ring.

Competition amongst bitches is very strong.

shows and perhaps other events. Wherever you go, you will always learn something new, and should be prepared to listen to any advice; many Whippeteers will be happy to help you.

If you are serious about taking up showing at the highest level, it is important to be honest with yourself and decide if your pet at home is really of the quality required to win. You may think seriously about buying another Whippet with showing particularly in mind – your pet will probably be delighted to have a companion.

Buying a Show Whippet

There are many options available to you if you are committed to buying a Whippet with showing in mind. You could return to the breeder of your pet, if they breed show dogs, and ask about a show quality puppy. It is strongly advisable to visit a few Whippet club shows, preferably championship shows, to watch the dogs and decide which of them you really like. You will be amazed at the vast array of colours as well as the look of the dogs that can be found, and it is important that you like what you see. Do not make any quick decisions, but you can enquire as to the availability of puppies in general.

If you are to visit a litter of puppies, or perhaps are thinking to consider an older one, it is fine to take someone with you who can advise on the finer points for showing if you don't feel confident going alone. This is a major decision and should be carefully thought through. Not only will you be buying a dog with a higher price tag, but later you will also be investing a lot of time and money in travelling to shows, paying entry fees and all the expenses incurred at shows, as well as adding another family member to your household. A breeder should be proud to sell a good quality show dog to you: it will be seen at shows so it is their reputation on the line.

Don't be afraid to ask about the good points, but expect the breeder to be honest enough to point out what they feel could be better. There is no such thing as a perfect dog, and a breeder, if they show themselves, will rarely sell their best stock, so you may have to compromise, and this is where an experienced companion is invaluable. It is to your advantage to know your dog's faults, so you are under no illusions. But if these are serious faults, would they compromise the Whippet's success in the ring? This may sound as if it is a minefield, and in some ways it is, but never be afraid to learn – and at the end of the day you have to live with your new purchase and enjoy it as much as your pet Whippet.

The Higher Levels of Showing

As you gain experience and confidence by attending your local shows, you will learn that there are different levels of show. A Companion Dog Show, which is where you started, is far removed from the large Championship Shows. You will be attending Limited Shows locally, which are restricted to dogs that have not won high awards at Championship Shows. So it is a good show to attend, and there will be a much more relaxed atmosphere. This type of show is often held in the local village hall, and the entry fees are reasonable; sometimes they are held in the evening, but usually at weekends. This is the type of show where everyone began to show their dogs, and they are especially good for puppies and/or the novice exhibitor to take part in.

The next level of local show is an Open Show, where you will perhaps see some champions exhibited. The general standard is high, and it is usual to have many specialist judges officiating, so there will probably be a few Whippet classes and perhaps a breed specialist as the judge. The class entries are higher, and you will be competing amongst other Whippets. It is normally a one-day show, but some societies run it over two days. Some Open Shows have a qualifier for Crufts, but this is mainly achieved at Championship Shows.

At the top level is the Championship Show. This show is usually held over anything from two to four days and can have an entry of up to 10,000, with all breeds of dog entered. Each breed is individually scheduled and will have a specialist judge. These judges have owned quality dogs and exhibited for many years. They may have been judging Whippets for many years, or it could be their first such appointment. This is a culmination of their breed experience, with success in the show ring as well as previous judging experience. This is normally the only level of show where you can qualify your Whippet for Crufts, and it is the only show where Challenge Certificates are on offer, and therefore the only shows where champions can be made. There are also Breed Club Championship Shows, where there will only be Whippets present, but the principle is the same. There may 150 to 200 Whippets entered.

To have a champion, your Whippet must have won three Challenge Certificates (commonly known as a C.C.) from three different judges. To be awarded a C.C. your Whippet has to be placed first in its breed class and remain unbeaten in subsequent classes. At the end

Ch. Rum Punch of Falconcrag and his daughter Ch. Becscott Standard Lady of Falconcrag.

Ch. Hammonds Sebastian.

Ch. Nothing Compares To You At Crosscop, Reserve Best in Show, Crufts.

of the male classes, all the first prize winners that are still unbeaten come into the ring and 'challenge' for Best Dog. The male that is declared the Dog C.C. winner is the best of all the males. There is also has a runner-up to that prize, known as a reserve C.C.; this is awarded to the second-best male in the judge's opinion. A Best Puppy male will also be declared.

At the end of the bitch classes the same process applies, and at the end of judging the Best Male and Best Female challenge each other for Best of Breed, and the two Best Puppies challenge for Best Puppy in Breed. These Championship Shows are held all over the country, and if you are interested to show at this level, it can become an expensive hobby. Many exhibitors travel to nearly every show both here and in other countries.

Here is a reminder of some of the important points to consider about showing your dog. There are many Whippets being shown, and the quality is high. If you are serious about showing regularly at all levels, it is imperative that you have a good quality Whippet. Buy a dog of the best possible quality that you can afford. It is an expensive 'hobby' and can become addictive. Be prepared to take advice, and be courteous whether you win or lose. You never stop learning. The judge's decision is final, win or lose – but remember, you are taking the best dog home!

Judging

Becoming a judge, at any level, is a recognition of your achievements both as an exhibitor and breeder. It takes many years of dedication to your breed before you can begin this journey, a point where your peers will respect your opinion, and indeed give you the honour of judging their dogs. It is said that it is not anyone's right to be a judge, it must be earned, but it can be the most rewarding thing you do, especially so in a hobby that you have dedicated yourself to.

To judge at The Kennel Club shows you must fulfil certain criteria to train to be a judge. The system is designed to encourage those who would like to judge, but also allows them to progress to whichever level they choose. Some judges only officiate in the breed they own, whereas other judges will expand their training and knowledge and judge different breeds. This is where the terms 'breed specialist' and 'non-breed specialist' come from. A breed specialist, as the title implies, is a judge who has personally owned and been involved with that breed, and usually has a string of successful dogs. For this reason their experience and knowledge are most valued by the exhibitors. They will judge with the finer points of the breed in mind, and often not only judge to breed type but also have a specific type within the breed that they prefer. This

Two judges decide the Best of Breed from the Dog and Bitch CC winners.

can often be similar to the Whippets they own themselves, but they also have the opportunity to reward other breeder types that they may admire.

A non-specialist judge may have had an association with the breed, or will have had years of mentoring and training by breed experts; they are no less qualified to judge, but may have a different outlook on the breed. The non-specialist judge tends to evaluate the exhibits in a more overall view, not having specific preferences as the breed specialist. This can mean that although the judgements of both judges are perfectly valid, they will often give a different result. This is viewed as healthy for a breed, as an experienced non-specialist can see the all-round picture and will not get fanatical about certain faults or points; it also makes the judging interesting to watch. However, it is important to note that all judges are required to report any health or potential health issues they see in a breed when they are judging.

A judge is also the custodian of the individual breeds, along with the owners and breeders, as it is considered that the placings they award illustrate what are the best in that breed, and that others should take heed of any points they make in their reports after the show. Judges at Kennel Club shows are required to judge by the show rules and to use the Breed Standard as a reference point when judging any breed. The Breed Standard is the blueprint that sets out the finer points that illustrate the

characteristics of a Whippet. Every breed recognised by The Kennel Club has a Breed Standard. As you will read later in Chapter 8, the Breed Standard is very detailed and gives the judge guidance. It should always be read before a judging appointment, and a copy is available at every show if needed.

How to Begin

After attending many shows as an exhibitor, you will begin to feel that you could perhaps be able to judge yourself. There are many things to learn as you train to be a judge, and one of the first and most important steps is to help at a dog show. This gives you an insight into what exactly makes a show run, and helps you to understand a judge's contribution in making the show a success. Show secretaries are extremely welcoming to anyone who can come along to help, as organising a show is a huge undertaking. The secretary would need to know what experience you already have, and would probably start you off by asking you to be one of the stewards in a judging ring. You would be working alongside the judge of the day and a more experienced steward, who will probably suggest what your duties will be. There is stewarding training available to view online on The Kennel Club website, which gives a basic indication of what is expected.

The main advantage to this is that you are gaining experience on how a ring works, and how it is managed, not only by the stewards but more importantly by the judge. You will be required to do several stewarding days, as this is one of the basic requirements that a judge needs to have fulfilled. There are seminars you need to do before you can judge, details of which are available from The Kennel Club.

Judging Whippets

To be a breed judge you will be required to attend a breed-specific seminar. These full-day seminars are run by breed clubs around the country in the course of each year. An experienced breed specialist gives a detailed talk on the finer points of the Whippet. This is based on the Breed Standard, with an extended instruction as to form and function. The speaker will usually have a live model to illustrate their talk, and there is also a question and answer time. Following this there is usually an opportunity to have a 'hands-on session' with experienced tutors, and a chance to ask questions.

This is only the first step in becoming a breed judge, and as much experience as possible should be gathered both judging and, if you are fortunate, being mentored by a breed expert. The next step to judging is to be invited to judge some Whippet classes, and this is where you are judging for real. It is an exciting time to be standing in the centre of the ring and bringing together your experience and love for Whippets. You will have to make many decisions, some easier than others, but as long as you judge with integrity and responsibility to Whippets as a breed, you will not go far wrong. It is an immensely rewarding experience, and you never fail to learn something new. Certainly nerve-racking to start with, understandably you will be nervous before you even start to judge, but if you have gained a good knowledge of the breed, you should be confident in what you are looking for and in being able to make your decisions in a professional manner.

As you judge more classes over time, you can progress to eventually achieving your ambition: to be a Championship Show judge. This is viewed as the ultimate accolade, and by this time you will have gained your judging experience and developed your own reputation as a judge whose opinion is valued.

It is advisable also to judge other breeds at lower levels if you have the opportunity to do so. This gives you a much broader outlook to your judging, and it also tests your knowledge and is good experience in judging something you are not so comfortable with. But whatever heights you decide to achieve as a judge, there is no better thrill than judging fabulous Whippets!

Judges Phil Moran Healy (Hillsdown) and Joachim Bartusch (of Gentle Mind) with their winners.

CHAPTER 8

The Whippet Breed Standard

The 'Standard of Excellence'

By the time that Whippets were taken up seriously as a showing breed, selective breeding was practised, albeit without pedigrees as far as we know. This selective breeding involved choosing parents that would produce functional dogs in the sport they were bred for. Whether the way they looked was incidental, or more probably a type was agreed on collectively as being successful, this type was to be nurtured and preserved for years to come. In the last 100 years no breeder is known to have had any puppies where a possible throwback to a mixed background has appeared, so it is safe to say that the Whippet is as pure as any other breeds.

The showing of dogs highlighted many native individual breeds, and The Kennel Club's responsibility was to find a way to preserve them along with the popular imported breeds. As far back as 1881, many breeds had a 'standard of excellence', and this was used by judges to evaluate the specific points for each breed. The total number of points was 100, and these were divided and allocated to parts of the dog, the number of points relative to their considered importance. There was no text supporting the points system, but it gives an indication as to how each part was valued.

Those who drew up these points would be judges of the day who were familiar with working dogs and how they should be built. The majority were stockmen who drew their knowledge from working with animals, and horses in particular. The horse has always had a close association with sighthounds, and so many terms have been transferred. The horse was also used in veterinary tuition as a model for student learning. Three 'breeds' that we are all familiar with, were listed together:

> **Greyhound:** Head 10 points, Neck 10 points, Chest and Forequarters 20 points, Loin and Back ribs 15 points, Hindquarters 15 points, Legs and Feet 15 points, Tail 5 points, Coat and Colour 10 points.
> **Lurcher:** Not shown or encouraged.
> **Whippet:** Same as the greyhound.

The Lurcher is still very popular today and bred very much for its purpose, but it was not regarded as a breed to be considered even as far back as 1881. The close relationship between the Greyhound and Whippet is recognised, and many thought the Whippet was a miniature Greyhound – so much so that at one point there was an attempt to rename the Whippet as such.

This standard clearly shows the emphasis on the chest and forequarters, which in practical terms is the area of the Whippet that allows it to be an efficient running dog. The chest has depth and shape that allows the heart and lungs to work to their maximum capacity within the ribcage. Sitting on the ribcage and attached by muscle, the forequarters are positioned to allow the running action of the shoulders, upper arm, legs and feet to function correctly and efficiently. The legs and feet themselves are graded with fifteen points, which recognises the importance of strong, well boned legs, pasterns and feet that cushion the action of the front and rear assembly when running over a variety of terrain.

Still as part of the functioning body, the loin and back ribs grade at fifteen points. The back ribs give length to the deep chest, extending the capacity of the chest but also supporting the spine as it extends into the loin area. The back ribs also support the underline from the chest and allow a gentle but definite tuck-up. The loin must allow the spine to flex when the Whippet is running, its strong muscle supporting the backbone as well as giving strength and a gentle rise to the topline, before it drops to the croup and hindquarters. The hindquarters have fifteen points, not as high scoring as the chest and forequarters, but as the powerhouse of the whole body, they have strength and power through well-developed muscling.

Under that muscle the bone structure must be firm and unwavering, but also the width of the hindquarters is vital to allow the hind legs to pass on each side of the shoulders as the Whippet gallops. The continuation of the spine is through the pelvis to the hindquarters. The tail, which is simply of good length, acts as a steering mechanism and for balance, and is valued at five points.

The remaining sections all have ten points each. The head should show quality of expression and a fineness of ears, as well as a fairly broad backskull to hold the functioning brain, wherein lies the ability to have thinking power. The length and strength of the head is important, and in particular the foreface. Attached to the head is the neck, which works in harmony with both the head and forequarters; it should be well muscled, of correct length, and have enough strength to hold any prey.

Coat and colour may seem insignificant, but due to the presence of Lurchers, Bedlington/Whippet and Collie crosses for example, it was necessary to stipulate those colours that were recognised in pure Whippets. Typically the coat is short, fine and close textured, and this emphasised the move away from allowing crossbred Whippets to be exhibited in the mid-1800s; some of these had wiry, rough-coated or semi-long hair, which was an indication of their mixed background.

So, even by just outlining the grading as in the points system, the underlying reasons for their different values show how these priorities were agreed on. This standard of excellence formed the basis of the Breed Standard that was eventually revised and established in a set format with the addition of descriptive text (*see* later in this chapter). The Whippet Breed Standard was drawn up at the request of The Kennel Club by a 'committee' of representatives of the Whippet clubs, and little has changed from that first standard to the current standard. However, there was one extremely important point that was missing, and which caused a positive discussion that all representatives agreed on, and that was the required height of a Whippet.

June Minns with Ch. Nimrodel Wanderer (left), and Editha Newton with Ch. Nutshell of Nevedith.

The Breed Standard has remained in place, and little has changed over the last 120 years or so, but one of the biggest changes was when The Kennel Club strove to bring the format into line with all Breed Standards. It was the opinion of many that in doing this, the essence of each individual breed lost a part of its important descriptive content. However, since that time amendments have been made periodically, and wording introduced to give a clearer and more precise understanding of what is required. The current standard is separated into headings where each part is described point by point; this is certainly more logical, and easier to commit to memory. However, one omission, in particular, which has not been replaced and is probably as relevant as the content itself, is the section on faults, identifying points that were not to be encouraged.

Faults

Weak, sloping or too straight pasterns, pigeon toes, tied elbows, loaded or bossy shoulders, wide on top and straight shoulder blades, flat sides. An exaggerated, narrow front is not to be encouraged.
Head and Skull: Appleskull, short foreface or downface.
Ears: Pricked or Tulip.
Mouth: Overshot or undershot.
Neck: Throatiness at the joint of the neck and jaw and at the base of the neck.
Body and Hindquarters: A short-coupled or cramped stance, an exaggerated arch, a camel or humped back (the arch starting behind the shoulder blades), a too short or overlong loin.
Tail: Gay, ringed or twisted, short or docked.
Coat: Wire- or broken-coated, a coarse woolly coat. Coarse thick skin.

Of course today, judges are asked not to fault judge, but to judge the Whippet as a whole and balance out the merits and demerits. This section was an important and useful part that perhaps should have been retained, as it highlights the fundamental faults that prevent a Whippet from being functional. The FCI Breed Standards in Europe do list faults in order of relevance down to eliminating points. We do not eliminate any exhibits in the UK in this way, but it is certainly useful for student judges to be made aware of them so that they can question their importance and hopefully recognise them.

Breed Type

Many of the established lines of early successful breeders have stood the test of time. England, as the country of origin of the breed, has upheld its responsibility to the Whippet, and many breeders and enthusiasts across the world have imported from the UK to form the basis of their own kennels. This has been of great benefit to these breeders, resulting in many great and successful kennels. The 'English' Whippet has passed on its many virtues and revolutionised its popularity around the world.

Ch. Simply A Lord, a lovely head study.

The breed is not only very strong numerically, but there is also a wealth of many beautiful specimens. In contrast to exports, very few Whippets up to the middle of the twentieth century have been imported. Previously, the quarantine laws meant six months of confinement for imports, not conducive to any sighthound character. However, due to the introduction of the pet passport there has been a great influx of different bloodlines more recently, which has been popular. Not only is there regular showing by UK exhibitors in Europe, but regular visits by European Whippet enthusiasts to this country has opened the competition in the show ring, and on the courses and tracks.

This exchange has in turn widened the breed's gene pool significantly. As always with imported stock, there is a settling down of type, and this has in some cases altered the look of some Whippets. This is not always a bad thing, as breeders should be looking to improve or add to their own bloodlines, and may feel it is necessary to import. The danger is that imports can bring too much diversity into a breed very quickly, and type can be diluted in such a way that the original type is only evident in the minority, or worse, becomes unrecognisable from that of its origins.

The Breed Standard is used by many countries around the world, although some do have their own versions, and this may be where some differences could occur. Many breeders in other countries based their bloodlines on English foundation stock originally, and the talents of breeders worldwide has revolutionised the Whippet mainly for the good – but the responsibility remains with the country of origin to uphold true breed type.

How do we define breed type? This is an opportunity to define the difference between breed type and type within the breed. Breed type is the combination of characteristics and quality that are brought together for that dog to be recognised as a Whippet. Type within the breed, or 'breeders' type' as it is often known, is shown by the depth of qualities in those characteristics with the additions of a consistency of looks or ability that can be recognised as originating from a breeding line or kennel. This consistency is carried through any offspring and can become sufficiently recognisable and dominant to be attributed to a certain breeder, very much like a family resemblance in humans. This is often the ultimate achievement in the eyes of a true breeder. They have, of course, the future of the breed in their hands.

The Whippet Breed Standard

(Reproduced by kind permission
of The Kennel Club)

Introductory Paragraph

A Breed Standard is the guideline that describes the ideal characteristics, temperament and appearance of a breed, and ensures that the breed is fit for function. Absolute soundness is essential. Breeders and judges should at all times be careful to avoid obvious conditions or exaggerations that would be detrimental in any way to the health, welfare or soundness of this breed. From time to time certain conditions or exaggerations may be considered to have the potential to affect dogs in some breeds adversely, and judges and breeders are requested to refer to the Breed Watch section of The Kennel Club website: www.thekennelclub.org.uk/events-and-activities/dog-showing/judging-dog-shows/breed-watch for details of any such issues. If a feature or quality is desirable it should only be present in the right measure. *However, if a dog possesses a feature, characteristic or colour described as highly undesirable it is strongly recommended that it must not be rewarded in the show ring.*

General appearance: Balanced combination of muscular power and strength with elegance and grace of outline. Built for speed and work. All forms of exaggeration should be avoided.

Characteristics: An ideal companion. Highly adaptable in domestic and sporting surroundings.

Temperament: Gentle, affectionate, even disposition.

Head and skull: Long and lean, flat on top, tapering to muzzle with slight stop, rather wide between the eyes, jaws powerful and clean cut. Nose black, in blues a bluish colour permitted, liver nose in creams and other dilute colours, in whites or parti-colour a butterfly nose is permissible.

Eyes: Oval, bright, expression very alert.

Ears: Rose-shaped, small, fine in texture.

Mouth: Jaws strong with a perfect, regular and complete scissor bite – that is, upper teeth closely overlapping the lower teeth and set square to the jaws.

Neck: Long, muscular, elegantly arched.

Forequarters: Shoulders well laid back with flat muscles. Moderate space between the shoulder blades at the withers. The upper arm is approximately of equal length to the shoulder, placed so that the elbow falls directly under the withers when viewed in profile. Forearms straight and upright with moderate bladed bone. Front not too wide. Pasterns strong with a slight spring.

Body: Chest very deep with plenty of heart room. Well filled in front. Brisket deep. Broad, well muscled back, firm, somewhat long, showing graceful arch over the loin but not humped. Ribs well sprung. Loin giving impression of strength and power. Definite tuck-up.

Hindquarters: Strong, broad across the thighs, with well-developed second thighs. Stifles well bent without exaggeration with hocks well let down. Able to stand naturally over a lot of ground.

Feet: Oval, well split up between toes, knuckles well arched, pads thick, nails strong.

Tail: No feathering. Long, tapering, reaching at least to the hock. When in action carried in a delicate curve not higher than the back.

Gait/movement: Should possess great freedom of action. In profile should move with a long, easy stride whilst holding topline. The forelegs should be thrown forwards and low over the ground. Hind legs should come well under the body giving great propelling power. General movement not to look stilted, high stepping, short or mincing. True coming and going.

Coat: Fine, short, close in texture.

Colour: Any colour or mixture of colours, except merle.

Size: Desirable height: Dogs 18.5–20in (47–51cm); bitches (17.5–18.5in (44–47cm).

Faults: Any departure from the foregoing points should be considered a fault, and the seriousness with which the fault is regarded should be in exact proportion to its degree and its effect upon the health and welfare of the dog.

Note: Male animals should have two apparently normal testicles fully descended in the scrotum.

Interpreting The Breed Standard

The true Whippet was bred to be a sporting dog and little else, so it is vital that the breed is preserved in type, construction and soundness. It is not only the judge's responsibility to reward the best specimens in accordance with the Breed Standard, but also any breeder or exhibitor should always consider whether the litter they plan, or the exhibit they show, is a true representative. A judge is reminded not to award prizes due to lack of merit, but to withhold them; likewise a breeder in showcasing their stock. In reality, it is extremely difficult to produce a really high quality specimen: it appears as a 'once in a lifetime' dog. A perfect dog has yet to be born, but if a compromise must be found it should be within the parameters of breed type and functionality.

We are fortunate that the Whippet remains a healthy breed, and its continuing participation in various disciplines may have a bearing on the prevention of health problems creeping in. With responsible breeding and attention to the control of exaggerations there is no reason for the Whippet to remain anything other than healthy. Of course, with the advancement of veterinary knowledge and the development of specific testing for various diseases, it has become more commonplace for health issues to be recognised.

Whilst this new-found information is useful, it should be put into perspective and dealt with in a sensible way. Breed Watch is now one of the main tools for health monitoring that The Kennel Club has in place. Judges are required to monitor health as they fulfil their appointments, and report on any issues found. Fortunately the Whippet is not one of the breeds categorised on Breed Watch, but it makes interesting reading to see what may happen if irresponsible breeding and exaggerations are ignored.

Over time fashions do change, and unfortunately it is inevitable that this encroaches into the breeding of Whippets. The breeder is responsible for ensuring this change is minimal, while the judge has the responsibility to ensure they do not award honours to a Whippet that lacks type, is of unsound construction and movement, or shows any indication of exaggeration.

The text of the Breed Standard is intended to be a concise description of how each breed looks, to enable the reader to apply this information and to judge if the points they are identifying are typical and desirable. This might be a judge, breeder, exhibitor or other interested readers. The words are carefully chosen so there is no ambiguity; however, each reader of the standard will interpret what they read in a different way, and will in turn give a different opinion. The following is an attempt to expand the original standard and to give some reasoning behind those words. Also included are the faults as listed in the early *'Breed Standard of Excellence'* inserted into the appropriate place: these are highlighted in italics for ease of identification.

General Appearance

The general appearance of the Whippet is of a medium-sized hound of moderate proportions. To remain balanced, the Whippet should be made up of four equal parts that function as a whole. Within each quarter, muscular strength and condition will supply the strength required for a running dog. The Whippet is built to run a short distance as quickly as possible, so it must be compact, but still retain the ability to flex and extend at a gallop. By design, history has dictated that the Whippet has a shape that is streamlined and aerodynamic from head to tail, and with that comes elegance and the grace of outline that is asked for. Being of moderate proportions, exaggerations will upset the balance if one or more of the points are overdone. The natural progression for exaggeration is for the whole dog to start to readjust and compensate in trying to redress the balance, and the result is that the whole Whippet becomes either untypical or unbalanced.

This shapely bitch is a good example of a Whippet's general appearance.

Characteristics

Characteristics that we have come to recognise are well known, and today the modern Whippet is much more of a companion than in the past. They are a useful size and have become a popular addition to any family. This adaptability has been the making of the breed, with their sculptured physique and air of importance, but being a loving and devoted companion as well. For those who choose to be actively involved in sport, the Whippet's inbuilt instincts give it this adaptability, and it needs no encouragement to be very competitive. It is important that this sporting ability is kept, and that the Whippet does not become a pet dog that lacks verve, inquisitiveness and character, and its raison d'être.

Head and Skull

One of the fascinating qualities in the group of dogs that are sighthounds is that they have a very similar head shape. All the breeds have long heads – this simply tells us that their heads are longer than they are wide. The shape of a Whippet head is rather like an arrow, with a broader skull and, as the standard says, 'tapering to the muzzle'. The only two sighthound breeds to have a skull width that is more than 50 per cent of the length of their head are the Whippet and the Italian Greyhound. However, in the Standard there is no mention of the proportions of the Whippet head, but it is generally accepted that the backskull and foreface should be of equal length. The width to the backskull allows plenty of brain power and dictates the position of the ears and

eyes. It also affects the shape of the eye and the depth of the stop.

The skull should be flat on top but appears slightly rounded and smooth. This is caused by muscle development on the top of the head. The sides of the skull should be smooth, with a slight muscle development, and the bone that runs from the corner of the eye to the ear, known as the zygomatic arch, should blend into the head and not stand out. A strong bone here makes the head too round in shape; it also alters the eye position to be at the front of the skull, and the eye shape becomes round, not oval.

The width between the eyes allows the Whippet to have good all-round vision, essential in a sighthound. The slight stop supports this width, and the gradual tapering down from the backskull to the muzzle allows a good width enabling strength, an efficient width to the nose for breathing, especially when galloping, and a strong, correct bite. The depth of the muzzle must be strong and clean cut with no excess lip, but must be in keeping with the shape of the head.

Faults: Appleskull, a short foreface or a downface.

Eyes

The position of the eye is on the outer edge of the skull, to enable clear panoramic vision as far as possible. The shape of the eye is described as oval, and this is dependent on its position. If the zygomatic arch is too prominent and strong, the eyes are more forward looking, therefore restricting the area of sight as well

Shaped like an arrow, the head tapers from the skull down to the muzzle.

The head is equal in length from the back of the skull (occiput) to the stop (between the eyes), and the stop to the nose.

The eyes are on a line with the ears.

The crowning glory of the head are the rose ears of fine texture.

as altering the eye shape to be round and sometimes more prominent. The eyes should never be round and bulbous.

There is no mention of eye colour in the standard and this is usually in keeping with the coat colour, but in reality, a darker eye is preferred as it gives a depth of character and a bright, intelligent expression. Light or yellow eyes are quite prominent and give a staring look, not the softer expression that is the Whippet's trademark. Wall eyes or part wall eyes sometimes occur in predominantly white-coloured Whippets as this is an extension of the coat colour into the eye. This would possibly affect their success in the show ring but is of no consequence otherwise. However, a wall eye is common in dogs that are merle in colour, and this coat colour is definitely not found in Whippets.

Ears

The crowning glory to any Whippet head is the desired 'rose ear'. This is an important breed feature that must be preserved. The ear is set in line with the outer corner of the eye. In the rose ear, the rounded part of the outer ear forms the shape of a rose; the size of this should be in keeping with the head, but is fairly small and unobtrusive. The outer flap of the ear is folded back when in repose, but when erect it forms the outer fold of the ear with a distinct fold that sits on top of the rose shape.

Characteristic of a correct ear is the fine texture: it should feel very smooth and pliable. It should be noted here that when alerted, a Whippet will lift its ears, and if very excited its ears may well become upright. This

is a normal movement; Whippets use their ears as well as their eyes when hunting. If you watch carefully, you will see them swivel their ears to assist them in locating prey. The ears should never be strong and stiff in texture so that they remain bolt upright when alert, and when in repose stick out straight behind the head, nor should they be large and heavy. They should also not be permanently upright and fluted, as a tulip shape. They should always return to a neat, folded ear set towards the back of the skull.

Faults: Pricked or tulip ears.

Mouth

The standard asks for a strong jaw, a complete, regular scissor bite. Strong jaws are vital for the Whippet to be able to kill and hold prey, but they should also be in harmony with the foreface, and not obtrusive. A complete set of teeth are the tools of the trade: any naturally missing teeth are a problem and can lead to a lack of teeth altogether, which is often hereditary. Missing, broken or discoloured teeth by trauma are very common and should not be viewed as a problem. A regular scissor bite indicates that the set of the jaw is correct. Well formed teeth of a good size are ideal.

An undershot jaw, where the lower jaw protrudes in front of the top jaw, is a hereditary fault, as is an overshot jaw: this is the reverse, where the top jaw protrudes further forwards and a gap appears between the tips of the top and bottom jaw. These faulty mouths mean that the Whippet is not able to formulate a firm bite, which is obviously a weakness.

Faults: Overshot or undershot jaw.

A complete set of good-sized, even teeth is essential.

A scissor bite, where the top teeth sit neatly over the bottom teeth; the premolars can also be seen.

Neck

In forming the link between the head and body, muscular strength is vital. The neck is a strong, muscular pillar that enables the head to be lowered to catch and hold prey, as well as allowing the Whippet to gain speed on the gallop by lengthening and keeping the Whippet balanced.

The length of the neck should be comparable to the length of the head. Too long, and the neck muscles lengthen, and in stretching become weakened. The neck becomes thin and elongated. If the neck is too short, the muscles are bulky and the neck loses its streamlined flat sides, as well as the ability to lift prey without breaking stride. The neck has a crest that is made by the vertebrae at the joint of the head and neck: this gives the elegant arch. Gently flowing down into the shoulders, there should be little resistance when your hand runs down it.

The point where the neck joins the body and is set into the front depends on the way the shoulders are angulated. A more upright front is usually indicated by a more upright neck, and a definite sharp angle joining at the shoulders. An over-angulated front shows the neck coming into the front at a lower point, and it looks bent in

towards the front; this is commonly called a 'ewe neck' as it is similar to the position of a sheep's neck.

It is important that the neck is fairly flat sided and streamlined without any excess skin as a dewlap or at

The neck is the same length as the head, nicely arched from the back of the head.

the base of the neck around the front of the body. The neck should also have good depth from the top line to the lower side of the neck.

Faults: Throatiness at the join of the neck and jaw, and at the base of the neck.

Forequarters

The shoulder blades are set on the ribcage and held by muscle, and the way they are angled depends on the shape of the ribcage. The shape of the ribcage should be oval, ensuring correct width to the front. The shoulder blade is a flat bone and lies with its broad end near the backbone. The top of the shoulder blade has two points: one is set lower than the backbone facing backwards, and this is known as the 'layback of the shoulder'. The other point is known as the top of the shoulder and is positioned in line with the backbone; it comes close to its corresponding blade on the other side at the withers. There should be a gap between these blades, again dependent on the shape of

the ribcage. This gap allows the head, neck and front to reach down when working.

The shoulder blade should be of a good enough length and angled to reach to the joint (the point of shoulder) where the bottom part of the shoulder blade meets the humerus (upper arm). The upper arm angles from this point of the shoulder back towards the elbow. It is of similar length to the shoulder blade, and this forms the front angulation. The angulation of the front allows the free movement of the shoulders, upper arm and legs in movement. It is worth noting here that the angle to the front is that of a sighthound, holding its head up with an eye on its target as it runs – the angulation is not as in other dogs, such as a working sheepdog, whose function is very different.

The standard asks for a bladed bone that is a specific type of bone peculiar to running sighthounds. In shape, the bone has a rounded front with a narrowing towards the back part of the leg. This is aerodynamic but also very strong. A round bone is too heavy, and a fine bone

Good layback of the shoulder blade with return of the upper arm allows a good forward reach in front. Both topline and underline are smooth and a flowing 'S' shape.

wouldn't support the rigours of galloping. The pastern should also be as strong and as broad as the foreleg above it, but shows as a slight spring, not upright, nor weak. The spring cushions the forequarters from being jolted and damaged on rough terrain.

Faults: Loaded or bossy shoulders – wide on top and straight shoulder blades, pigeon toes. An exaggerated narrow front is not to be encouraged. Tied elbows. Flat sides. Weak, sloping pasterns or pasterns that are too straight.

Body

As stated earlier, the chest is oval. The oval shape is made by the ribs coming down from the backbone and 'springing' out. This spring of rib allows room for the heart and lungs to function to their full capacity, and stretches around two-thirds of the way down the ribs. The depth of chest is made up by the next one-third, which comes slightly inwards to form the base of the oval shape and not only gives depth to the brisket, but can be seen at the front as fill-in of the forechest.

The back of the Whippet is broad, strong and muscular. The topline from behind the shoulders slowly begins a gentle rise, which gives the arch over the loin. It is important that this arch starts in the correct place to ensure the Whippet remains correctly balanced. A very short-coupled body will lead to the topline being too exaggerated, and it will look humped or wheel-backed: this is as undesirable as a back that is too long. Long loin muscles stretch and weaken, and the back flattens out both standing and on the move. The correct length of the loin is very important, as it allows the back to flex when at full gallop. The loin is the only part of the backbone where there is no other support than muscle, so it must be extremely strong and well developed. The rise over the loin is made by the development of this muscle.

Faults: A short-coupled or cramped stance, an exaggerated arch, a camel or humped back (the arch starting behind the shoulder blades), a too short or overlong loin.

Hindquarters

There may be room for misinterpretation in the phrase 'Able to stand over a lot of ground', and it may be that this has encouraged the preponderance of an exaggerated

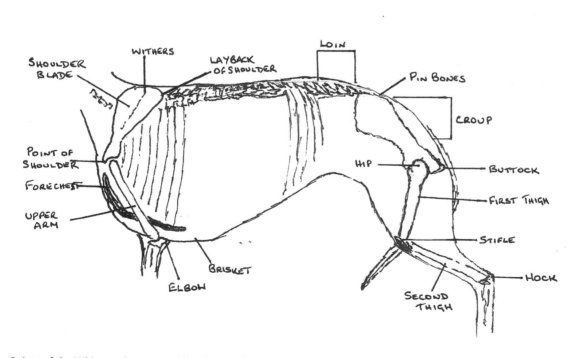

Points of the Whippet that are used in the Breed Standard description.

hind angulation. The look of a Whippet standing with long, sweeping hindquarters in many eyes is flashy and exciting, but the truth is that this is not functional, and causes an imbalance and a weakness. A Whippet should stand over the ground in a balanced and stable way that enables the front construction to allow legs and feet to be positioned well under its body; it should not give the impression of being tacked on at the front, or be in a rocking-horse position. The hindquarters should be broad and also give stability, so they allow free movement but also support the pelvis. When viewed from the back, this is an echo of the width of the pelvis. This width enables the hindlegs to drive forwards, especially when galloping, as the hindlegs come forwards on either side of the shoulders.

The top thigh or first thigh on the hindlegs should be well developed with strong muscles; this is also flat muscle and is well defined and not rounded or bulbous. The stifle joint is well bent, continuing the gentle curves of the body, but as the standard says, it should be without exaggeration. The length from the stifle joint to the hock joint should be in keeping with the overall balance of the Whippet. The muscle here is the second thigh: it should be well developed, and the length here is important. If the second thigh is too short, the hindquarters will not be able to drive forwards in conjunction with the first thigh. In contrast, if the second thigh is too long, the muscle lengthens and begins to stretch and weaken. This in turn affects the stability of the hocks, and causes a deviation in the way they support the hindquarters.

The hindquarters are strong and well muscled. A line from the buttock to the front of the hind feet confirms balanced, unexaggerated hindquarters. The back leg from the hock to the ground should be straight.

Feet

The shape of the foot may not seem to be important, but it is essential that it is correctly made. The foot is oval – that is, slightly rounded with rise to the knuckles, with the centre two toes slightly longer than the outside toes. This type of foot is able to open and close when on ground of varying types, to maximise grip and to enable the Whippet to turn and gallop. A shorter foot is usually too round, and all the toes are of similar length – and with shorter toes the flexibility of the foot is lost; this conformation often goes together with upright pasterns that have no spring, and therefore no cushioning for the front.

The opposite to a short, round foot is an open, flat foot. This is arguably the worst fault in a foot. The toes are splayed out flat with no arch to the toes, the pads are thin, and the pasterns are usually at a 90-degree angle to the foot, and totally dysfunctional. In the correct oval foot, the pads are thick, as in wearing well-soled shoes. The nails play a crucial part in the function of the foot, as they can be extended and used to grip the ground; it is therefore correct to have nails that are well kept – not too long but equally not too short.

Tail

Firstly, let us deal with feathering on the tail. The standard states 'no feathering', as this eradicates the acceptance of mixed blood in the breed. Many of the sighthound breeds do have feathering on their tails, so the standard directly removes this trait. Although smooth-coated, the Whippet does have slightly longer hairs on the underside of the tail. This is not classed as feathering, which is much longer and affects the shape of the tail. The tail itself is fairly broad as it leaves the body, and tapers to a fine point; this point should reach at least to the point of the hock, although some do have longer tails. A Whippet with a naturally short tail is often too compact or unbalanced in the rest of its body. The tail acts as a rudder in helping to steer the Whippet when it is turning when galloping.

The Whippet also uses its tail to show its feelings, and will draw it up high between its legs if it is unsettled in any way; and as mentioned earlier, if it is asserting its authority, it will raise its tail quite high. As it moves into a trot the tail will be raised out past the hocks; if the tail is set correctly from the croup, it is impossible for it to come over the back. The shape of the tail is strong at the root, tapering with a gentle curve towards the tip. It should not be ringed or have kinks.

Faults: Gay, ringed or twisted, short or docked.

Gait or Movement

With everything in the correct proportion and balance, the Whippet should be a sound mover in a breed-typical way. Any exaggerations have a direct impact on movement. A Whippet is a compact, streamlined running machine. Firstly, at a trot – as seen in the show ring or out for a brisk walk – the front movement comes from

The oval feet should be well split up between the toes, which allows them to open and close when galloping.

Forward reach from the shoulder allows a low, daisy-cutting action. The topline is firm and the hindquarters drive with strength and freedom.

the shoulder, extending through the legs and feet to allow the forelegs to reach forwards with a low 'daisy-clipping' action. The knees should not be lifted high, nor should the 'reach' start from the elbow: the whole of the front construction is used. In harmony, the hindquarters drive from the hips through the stifle and hock to the hind foot. This action brings the hind foot forwards under the body and almost into the place where the corresponding front foot has just lifted. That foot uses the ground to drive the hindleg back, giving power to the forward reach. As the front and back legs work in harmony, the body holds the whole flowing, moving action together.

The body being strong and 'together' is the anchor for a smooth, easy stride and holds the arch to the topline. With the correct oval ribcage and the broad hindquarters, movement in front and back should be true, showing good width. The width to the front should be the same from the forechest down to the feet. The width to the rear should be from the haunch bones down through the stifles to the hock and on to the feet, without any deviation from the true. It should be noted here that the Whippet will move with its hindquarters slightly in from the standing position, but they should never be narrow or converging.

The Breed Standard is not the document for describing the way in which all these points come together when the Whippet is running. It is a descriptive text that outlines the conformation that enables the Whippet to be breed typical. With that in mind, here is a description of the way in which a Whippet gallops. To move from a walk to a trot the Whippet will lead from one side and extend its right front foot – for example, at the same time the left hind foot will move forwards to drive the hindquarters, and this foot lands very near to where the left front foot has just been lifted and is now thrown forwards; the right hind foot is extended out behind. This continues in harmony and is a sort of diagonal gait. At this speed the position of the Whippet's head

Front movement with good width, true with no deviation.

is not as important as when it is galloping; however, the fashion of holding up the Whippet's head by the lead causes an unnatural lifting of the head and can disrupt the smoothness of gait – and often a handler's tight hold can lead to unstable front movement and can unbalance the Whippet.

As the Whippet increases its speed, breaking into a slow gallop and then to a racing speed, it will lower its head as the reach of the neck increases in length to gather speed. One hind leg will start the gallop by pushing off as the Whippet leaps into a gallop. The opposite hind foot hits the ground as the first is lifted, and there comes a point where the Whippet is not touching the ground at all: this is the point where the long suspension of the Whippet occurs. The opposite front leg to the hindleg that started the leap comes to the ground: at this point the front is cushioned by the spring in the pastern. As that front leg moves back, the opposite front leg hits the ground, at which point the hindlegs drive forwards to a point on either side of the front shoulders: therefore there must be plenty of width to the hindquarters, and equally this is why the front should be narrower than the rear. The loin is flexed allowing the maximum springing action and strength of the whole body to be utilised. At this point both front legs are off the ground, as are the hindlegs: a suspension gallop.

As momentum is gathered the wave of power continues, and the weight of the body being moved forwards increases the speed. Any deviation from the galloping line is steered by the head and neck, and assisted by the tail acting as a rudder. When the gallop ends, often abruptly, the momentum carries the body on, and the head, neck, feet and nails as well as the tail all play a part in bringing the body to a stop.

Coat and Colour

In the early days of the Whippet, the move to the purebred Whippet from its predecessors influenced the way it looked. As mentioned earlier, the fact that there have been no known throwbacks shows how successful this move was. A dominant feature in mixed breeding is often the wrong type of coat appearing in a litter of puppies. The coat should be of fine texture, close and sleek, and is undoubtedly the easiest of coats to keep clean. However, the length of the actual individual hair can vary, with whites often having a slightly longer length, whilst brindles often have very short hair. The tail hair is of two types, a slightly longer hair on the underside of the tail, but it should not be so long as to be described as feathering.

Nearly all colours or mixtures of colour are allowed, but there are some colours that are not breed typical: black and tan, liver or blue merle would be of mixed

The first suspension of the gallop. One front foot is beginning to drop to the ground. The position of the head indicates 'hunting by sight'.

Completing the double suspension: broad hindquarters allow the hindlegs to come down on each side of the shoulders.

The tail acts as a steering aid, and the toes open to gain maximum grip.

blood. There are many colours of Whippet, and this is often a decider when choosing a Whippet for yourself. There are blacks and blues, which some breeders specifically breed for, and have their specific bloodlines. Fawns and brindles are the most popular colours seen, and particolours and whites are especially appealing.

Faults: Wire or broken-coated, a coarse, woolly coat, coarse thick skin.

The nose should be black, while in blues a bluish colour is permitted; in creams the nose is liver, and in other dilute colours, in whites or parti-colours, a butterfly nose is permitted. For those interested in the colour breeding of Whippets – or more specifically blacks, blues and creams – this is a pigmentation colour in keeping with these dominant and recessive colours.

Size

The desirable height in dogs should be 18½–20in (47–51cm), whilst in bitches it should be 17½–18½in (44–47cm).

There is often debate on this subject, and there is now a tendency for taller dogs to be the norm, particularly bitches. It should be noted that the Whippet started out as a small, useful-sized dog, and within the sighthound family there is little between the maximum and minimum

heights of different breeds, and with that characteristics change. The very characteristics that give breed type can easily be lost, as we discussed earlier in the history of the breed. If the breeders and judges ignore this fact the Whippet will disappear. Throughout the history of the Breed Standards held by The Kennel Club, there have been discussions as to whether the height limits should be raised: this was being discussed at the beginning of the 1950s, according to C.H. Douglas Todd. Nutrition and 'fashions' meant a taller Whippet was more popular. This argument has been strongly defeated on numerous occasions, with only a small change in more recent years, a decision lamented by many.

So it seems strange that the descriptive words that apply to the Whippet – 'moderate' and 'medium sized' – are not in the General Appearance section of the Standard. In other disciplines height and weight can be very important as a restriction or a qualifier when taking part in sport classes. The Greyhound that won the Waterloo Cup in 1887 and 1888, 'Coomassie', was said to measure 24in (60cm) at the shoulder, a clear 3in (7.6cm) smaller than today's standard height of the Greyhound. Also one of the first Whippet bitch champions, Ch. Manorley May from the mid-1890s, was recorded as being 17in (44cm).

Measured traditionally from the withers to the ground between 17½–20in (44–51cm), the Whippet sits between the larger Greyhound, whose height is between 27–30in (69–76cm), but closer to the smaller Italian Greyhound, measuring between 12½–15in (32–38cm), and is defined within this very strict height limit. The tendency is for Whippets to be 'up to size' or to err on the higher limits today, a more correct, 'standard' Whippet taking on characteristics similar to the smaller Italian Greyhound; these are seldom seen, particularly in the show ring. This is probably due to the popularity of a more impressive 'big is beautiful'.

Looking back when Whippets were, in general, fitting the lower limits of the standard heights, the head type was shorter and the backskull more pronounced, the back more arched, overall the bone was of finer substance, and movement was more towards a higher stepping, shorter stride than today's Whippet's long, easy stride. This long stride belongs to bigger breeds, not to the Whippet, and the Breed Standard is very specific about describing typical movement. A Whippet that stands over 20in (51cm) at the shoulder will begin to show characteristics of a Greyhound. Although of similar proportions and a similar shape, the Greyhound head has a longer head in overall length, to be in keeping with the overall size of the dog, and the skull becomes less pronounced with a slight reduction in the depth of the stop.

As pointed out earlier, only two breeds of Sighthound, the Whippet and the Italian Greyhound, have a width of skull measuring over 50 per cent of the length of head. This means the back of the head is more pronounced than the foreface. The Whippet holds its head forwards and slightly higher than the line of its shoulders, whereas the position of the Greyhound's head is much higher. To remain in balance, the neck and body of a Greyhound are longer, as is the length of leg, therefore the height is increased. The essential 'handiness' of the Whippet size becomes compromised, and this in turn affects the ability to retain the sharpness and style of a fast, sharp, short-distance sprinter. The style in which it gallops changes to a longer, loping gallop. A simple question might be this: would you be able to carry a Greyhound under your arm?

So it is easy to understand why an increase or decrease in size is very detrimental to breed type. It is natural that the proportions also increase or decrease to remain balanced, and all other characteristics must follow suit. If

Breed type: from left to right: an Italian Greyhound, a Whippet and a Greyhound.

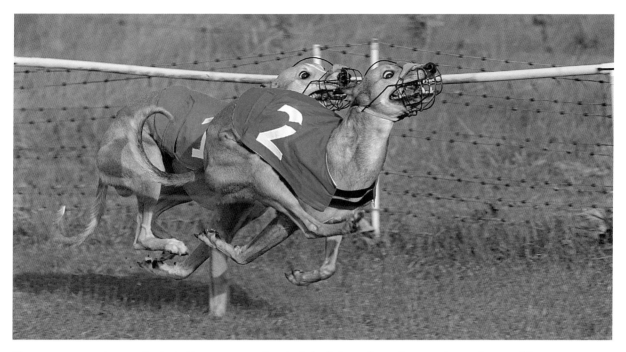

The eagerness can be seen in the Whippet's eyes as its whole body is used to gain as much speed as possible.

they do not, the Whippet becomes unbalanced and not as appealing to the eye, and more importantly, it will also become dysfunctional, therefore removing the reason for which it was originally bred.

Faults

The Standard says: 'Any departure from the foregoing points should be considered a fault, and the seriousness with which the fault should be regarded should be in exact proportion to its degree and its effect upon the health and welfare of the dog.'

Note: Males should have two apparently normal testicles fully descended in the scrotum. In the past there have been problems with cryptorchidism (no testicles evident) or monorchidism (one testicle evident) in the breed – a hereditary fault – so it is important that this check is done. In very young male puppies, the testicles may not always be fully dropped, and they can draw them up if they feel anxious. A judge would use their discretion in this instance.

The early show Whippets had the advantage in that they were drawn from the core of working and racing dogs. Selectively bred, by the time they appeared in the show ring, breeders were using their skills often learnt from rearing stock animals to produce champions. Early pedigrees show that these breeders were increasingly using 'line breeding' to concentrate the desired features that ensure breed type. A quality of type is evident in most of the early show dogs, very comparable with Whippets of the present day. Of course, not all Whippets are show dogs, but most are registered initially by The Kennel Club.

One of the greatest qualities of the Whippet is that in general there is not a great discrepancy in types, and often many dogs can be multifunctional, as many racing or lure-coursing dogs are also show dogs. Many dogs have champion titles in more than one discipline. However, probably the racing Whippet *is* the truest to the original type. In lure coursing there are different criteria, whereas in agility and obedience, for example, it is all about ability and performance.

CHAPTER 9

Racing and Lure Coursing

Racing – The True Origin

Racing is clearly an important part of the original function of the breed, and the source of the modern-day Whippet. There is no doubt the Whippet went from strength to strength, gaining popularity during the nineteenth century. Whilst there was an effort to popularise racing in the south of England, it was predominantly in the northern counties that meetings were held. There are accounts of how the racing Whippets were trained and reared for what was eventually known as 'old-time Whippet racing'.

The Whippet was reared within the family, and each family member would have a part to play in the development of their Whippet to produce a top quality running dog. Even if the family were on the edge of poverty, their racing dog would be fed on the best meat available. C.H. Douglas Todd says in his book *The Popular Whippet*: 'They were not even fed with ordinary beef which would be obtained from the butcher's shops. Some of the best dogs fed exclusively upon Scotch Beef which was sent down specially for them.'

The Whippet's training was very intense and specialised. Like any Whippet, the racing Whippet was trained in basic manners so it could live in the home, then as it grew it was introduced to more formal training. It was trained to focus on the 'rag' from an early age, and often this would be in the form of games with the children of the family. The Whippet would be encouraged as it gained weight and speed to take part in trial races, along with youngsters of a similar age until it was fully ready to compete.

The starting of the race was full of excitement, and great skill was demonstrated by the slippers. These slippers were the men who held the Whippet at the starting line of the race. The Whippets were held by their collar or scruff of the neck in one hand and their hindquarters or root of their tail by the other. On the sound of the starting pistol the slippers would literally throw the Whippets along the track as far as they could, often ending up flat out on the ground themselves. The Whippets would run towards the finishing line where their owners were shouting, whistling and shaking the 'rag' in encouragement. As the Whippets approached the end of the race, they would often launch themselves at their owners and be spun round as they grabbed the rag – such was their enthusiasm for getting their 'prey'.

Many of the Whippet's present characteristics were developed at this time, and their adoption by more upper-class owners clearly helped the breed's cause. However, Whippet racing still struggled to make an impact in the South. Even an attempt to increase the popularity of Whippet racing on 8 June 1895 by The Ladies Kennel Association at Ranelagh Club grounds at Barn Elms, London, fell short of elevating the breed. The Ladies Kennel Association's championship show is now part of the busy show calendar, but this was their first flagship show, run entirely by women. It was advertised in the earlier Crufts catalogue thus:

Slippers let the racers go, often landing flat on the ground to get the best start. The Lord Lonsdale Cup race on 13 June 1930 in Cardiff.

The latest London sport, Whippet racing, will be a feature. The event is to be attended by the Prince and Princess of Wales (King Edward and Queen Alexandra) and their daughters.

Although predominantly a northern pastime and not fashionable for many, the organisers had given the sport of Whippet racing a platform by hosting this event. It had to be perfect as royalty was present, so the highly regarded racing dogs and their entourage were brought down from Lancashire and Yorkshire. One of the notable stewards overseeing the racing was James Bottomley of the famous Manorley kennel. Suitably briefed as to their conduct and not wanting to have raised voices and loud whistles within earshot of the royals, they were instructed always to maintain decorum.

At the usual race meets, the Whippets would be held by a slipper and their owners would be at the finishing line, normally shouting encouragement, blowing whistles and waving rags to entice the dogs to run towards them, adding to the excitement of the dogs wanting to burst from their slippers, barking and screaming – the noise would build up to a loud crescendo. However, at the Ladies Kennel Association's championship show it was considered uncouth for the attendees to act in such a way in view of their royal visitors, so no shouting or

Trialling a youngster with one faster and one slower Whippet.

the place until they spied their owners, and then raced up the track towards them. However, chaotic as it must have been, Whippet racing eventually caught on, and regular racing became popular. Queen Alexandra herself became a Whippet owner and a staunch supporter of the breed.

Under the Measure

In Newcastle and surrounding areas of Durham, the handicaps were decided by measuring the Whippets. There was a big discrepancy in the sizes of Whippets presented for racing by their owners, so to establish a handicap system, the Whippets were categorised by height, and so measuring was introduced. This was not without its 'problems', as owners tried to inveigle the inspectors into getting their dog an advantage in handicap. The measuring stick had a nail or similar pin on the mark of the height limit. Many owners taught their dogs to dip their shoulders to avoid being pricked by the nail or pin, and miraculously came under the measure! This was soon replaced by a different technique, and each dog was laid down on its side and measured from the top of the shoulder to the pad of the foot.

whistles of encouragement were allowed on that day. The Whippets were looking for their own rag so they could run towards the voice they knew, and added to this, the starting pistol was also muffled to give out a less frightening bang. So the confused Whippets ran all over

Further south in Lancashire and Yorkshire the Whippets were weighed, and handicapped in relation to their weight, bearing in mind the broader spectrum of the weights of the smooth-coated Whippets; this would seem to be a fairer criterion. These breeders were

The lure is distanced from the Whippets to keep them keen, but not near enough to be caught.

fine tuning a racing dog, but sadly we presume with no pedigrees as such – the benchmark used was probably that of choosing a male for stud that had the performance and 'good looks', and putting it to a fast, good producing bitch.

At its height in the years before World War I, Lancashire was one of the most popular counties for Whippet racing. Some race meets were hosted at the Borough grounds in Oldham, fielding an astounding 300 dogs in one handicap. Other notable tracks included Higginshaw and Wellington Grounds in Bury, also well attended. These popular meetings must have attracted the attention of those who were also interested in the opportunity of showing, and generated an acceptable outlet for 'slower' dogs; this was an ideal situation for those in racing circles. The show goers also had the benefit of buying a readymade prospect.

Unfortunately the sport suffered a setback during the war years, and its popularity waned as there were more pressing matters, but an effort to revive the sport in its original form was undertaken by C.H. Douglas Todd of the Wingedfoot Whippets. However, his intention of returning this 'old-time' Whippet racing to its former popularity was met with criticism, and he made these observations:

> I am quite sure that all the old-time Whippets used to move with a definite highstepping hackney action in spite of all we say about the movement restricting speed. I am also certain that no Whippet starting from 'boxes' (traps) as they do, could have lived with a good dog of the old days being 'thrown' by a first rate

The front racer starts to use his ears as an extra sense.

All the racers now have their ears erect and alert.

slipper. I am just as confident that it was the betting on the dogs which led to the pastime falling into disrepute.

His contemporaries were of the same opinion, and not wishing to support a seedy gambling sport, discouraged any idea of its revival.

The Art of Racing

Although this type of 'rag' racing did continue in a small way, it was soon overtaken by an updated version of more organised racing. The sport of Whippet racing was taking on a new look, with the dogs released from traps and chasing a moving lure, very similar to what you would see on a Greyhound racing track. The traps are open-fronted with bars for the dogs to see out of, and most traps have a door to the rear to put the Whippet inside the trap. The lure is a rag, a plastic bag, a rabbit skin or something similar, tied securely on to a long rope. In the early days the rope with lure attached was wound round the wheel of an adapted bicycle with the 'rider' pedalling to wind up the rope and make the lure 'run'.

The lure operator's job is very specialised because they must be able to judge the Whippets speed in relation to the lure's distance from the racing Whippets. The lure operator is usually sited about halfway down the track so they can estimate the speed of the lure. The lure must be distanced so it is close enough to the Whippets that they can see it and want to chase it, but also sufficiently far from the runners for the duration of the race that they don't catch it. At the start of the race, the lure runs past the traps, and at a given point the traps are opened simultaneously by a starter pulling a handful of ropes attached to the trap doors. The dogs begin to race down the track towards their owners who are standing at the finish line. In contrast to those early days, the races are run in total silence: no one is allowed to make a sound as the dogs race.

Any handicaps were managed by where each trap was placed in relation to the start line; this depended on the weight-to-distance ratio, so the dogs with the higher

Tussling for position but never taking their eyes off the lure.

The feet on the right-hand-side Whippet are open so it can use its nails. The tail is steering.

The final moment, head stretched forwards.

Prising the jaws away from the 'catch'.

handicap would start further back. At the end of the race the Whippets usually caught the lure and their jaws had to be prised open to let it go, such was their determination. As racing developed the lure was eventually modified and was run by a car battery; now it is by a bespoke motor. The Whippets get very excited as they are put into the traps, and this increases as they hear the lure start to move. The track is either straight and 150 to 175 yards long, or it has one large curve and is 220 yards long. The track surface is of short, mown grass, and is not of the cinder-track variety of years ago.

Establishing Formal Racing

Whippet racing became an extremely popular sport with racing clubs all over the country. The clubs were mainly open to all and known as non ped(igree). This allowed all Whippet types to take part; they did not have to be of pure blood, nor did they need to be registered with The Kennel Club. The reason for this was that the sport was established long before the pedigree Whippet was recognised by The Kennel Club, and many racing dogs were of a Whippet type and so could compete together.

In October 1968 The British Whippet Racing Association (BWRA) was founded. It brought together many clubs and supported them in their regional activities, as well as bringing some standardisation of rules to the sport. The BWRA enabled all Whippet types to compete, and they were regulated by being within the parameters of their type and size. Racing clubs that are affiliated to the BWRA are controlled by the registering of dogs that have met the scrutiny of the registrar. They have a height limit of 21in for both dogs and bitches and a weight limit of 32lb, with an allowance of 4oz either side of this. Each Whippet is weighed at every meeting. There was also a Yorkshire League of Whippet Racing that operated from 1965 to 1975, in which ten racing clubs took part.

The popularity of Whippet racing increased because of the different types of Whippet that were allowed to run, often with mixed backgrounds. Up until that time The Whippet Club had only been involved in the pure-bred Kennel Club-registered, showing side of Whippets. They felt that their objective of preserving the purebred Whippet was in danger of being compromised, and as being the parent club of the breed, the committee voted to establish a racing association. The Whippet Club Racing Association (WCRA) was established in 1970

for purebred Kennel Club-registered Whippets, and was the first of its kind. Soon many regional pedigree clubs popped up and became affiliated to this association. Working on the same lines as the BWRA, it was able to promote a fit-for-function breed with a registration process of inspection and issuing passports, which, like our own passports, identified each Whippet. This identification is quite a lengthy process, to ensure that the background of the Whippet is correct.

Once a Whippet is accepted by a club secretary, they can begin trials and can then start the passport process. Both the breeder of the dog and another 'supporter' have to verify to the club registrar that the details that form the application are correct to the best of their knowledge, and that in their opinion the five-generation pedigree is correct. It is up to the registrar to issue a passport; they may query any part of the process, depending on appearance or doubtful pedigrees, and will investigate any case where a breeder has falsely registered a puppy or litter. The registrar is vastly experienced and can often highlight any discrepancies. The difference between the two associations is not huge and their operating methods are very similar, but the distinction between the purebred Kennel Club racing Whippet and the non ped. racing Whippet may not be in their looks but is certainly in their pedigrees.

There have been many Whippets that have competed in the show ring, have raced and also coursed, and this is a tribute to the preservation of the breed with its many characteristics and its good temperament. This has allowed Whippets to participate successfully in all three disciplines, although there is no crossover in the disciplines today. The one thing that is not so evident in the breed is any vast difference within types, which over the years has developed in breeds such as show and working gundogs. Many show gundogs achieve their titles in the ring and in the field, but there can be a big difference in the way they look – as, for example, between a working and a show Cocker Spaniel.

To their credit, this preservation must be attributed to the two racing associations that regulate the Whippet racing sport, ensuring that the height and weight limits remain in context to the original purpose of the Whippet. There are slight differences in the build and substance in some, as you would expect a finer, more lightly built dog to have a turn of speed to race, as opposed to a show Whippet that is in show condition and carrying more weight. Those original Whippets, the true foundation for the breed, came from racing tracks or were bred from racing stock, so it is not unusual that this legacy continued through the pedigree breeding and dominant kennels that went on to have multipurpose successful lines.

Exploring Whippet Racing

A lot of specialised effort goes into breeding a racing Whippet, and breeders would probably not freely sell a racing dog to a beginner. The best way to progress would be to attend race meetings and talk to those who take part, so you begin to learn the 'trade'. It is a very exciting sport, but as with any event it takes a lot of organising. It may help you to involve yourself with this side of racing by offering to help at an event. This will be greatly appreciated, and over time you will be recognised as having a true interest; this will be looked on favourably, and you may be asked to participate more fully.

Often it is by chance that you will be offered a puppy or a more experienced racer. It is very fortunate for you if this happens, and is a very important starting block for you. The breeders of racing dogs are very specific in the lines they breed with speed in mind. As explained in the section on finding a puppy, deciding on what you would like to do with your Whippet may have pointed you in this direction. Most people at race meetings are very friendly, and it is a great family outing. You can gain a lot of knowledge by attending and learning from others, but it is you who will have to put in the hard work to train and maintain your Whippet to compete well.

Normally you would not be allowed to race your Whippet until it has reached the age of between six to twelve months, depending on the club's criteria, but there are trials and opportunities for younger dogs to take part without damaging their immature bodies and legs. Trialling begins with your Whippet being tested between a faster and a slower Whippet. Your Whippet must not turn its head to the other runners on three occasions. To compete in an Open meeting, you will need to have a passport for your dog. To make a racing champion, two wins at Affiliated Nationals or WCRA events are required. The best introduction is always to go to

At full stretch, the hindquarters at their maximum, the hindfeet flexed in a gallop.

an event and see it for yourself – take advice, but more importantly enjoy the experience.

Lure Coursing

The very reason that sighthounds were developed was to hunt by sight and to 'course' their prey. As mentioned previously, the prey that was available depended on the country of origin, the terrain, and the hunter's requirements. In England, the Greyhound was used traditionally to hunt hares and the Whippet to catch rabbit. The Greyhound was the sighthound of the nobility, and the Whippet the working man's pride. The nobility would take their Greyhounds to hunt, and the thrill of the course was watching the hound work in twists and turns chasing the hare until it was caught and killed. The Whippet worked in exactly the same way, but its quarry was smaller, and after the course and kill, the rabbit was taken home to eat. But the enjoyment of the Whippet owner was no less than that of the nobleman, and these sports continued until quite recently.

The famous Waterloo Cup, a Greyhound coursing event, was known worldwide. The Whippet was never recognised in the same way as the Greyhound, but in time its capabilities were also extended to course the hare, and in 1962 the Whippet Coursing Club was established. There is a very detailed description of Whippet coursing and how it operated in Mary Lowes' book *The English Whippet*. It is a thorough account of this branch of the Whippet's function. She emphasises that there have been Whippets that have been successful in the coursing field as well as the show ring, as have her own 'Nimrodels'.

Coursing hare was made illegal by the Hunting Act of 2004, which stipulated that the hunting of hare with dogs was not allowed – which rang alarm bells. The Act stipulated that hunting with two dogs or more having flushed out game was not allowed, and this could be any owner of two or more Whippets who put up anything when out walking! It is problematic to undo the centuries of hunting instinct in any sighthound. An alternative sport had to be developed that encompassed this type of work, and led to the definite establishing of lure coursing as a sport for sighthounds in the UK; it has now become very popular, and a vast array of different breeds take part in it and fully enjoy it.

Lure coursing is an organised event in which a lure made of nylon rope with plastic strips attached, is laid out with a series of pulleys. The pulleys are positioned so the lure moves in a zigzag fashion that imitates the darting and changes of direction a hare would make if it were being coursed. So it is very different to the straight or gently curved tracks seen in racing. This is a very natural process for the Whippet, and tests their skills at twisting and turning, which they have done for hundreds of years. The lure can be one of a continuous type that is effectively one large circle and is pre-set for each run, or it can be a length of rope that drags the lure to a certain point and is returned to the start for every run.

This type of lure coursing has developed and become popular in the USA. At the 1995 First Whippet Congress there was a trip on the last day, Sunday, to watch the Whippets take part in this sport. Many UK enthusiasts were present, and enjoyed the prospect of an entertaining day watching the excited Whippets doing what they loved. And love it they did! The first lure-coursing club established in the UK was the British Sighthound Field Association (BSFA), which as its name implies was open to all sighthound breeds. Other clubs have followed as the sport has increased in popularity, and many now specialise in one breed.

The Sporting Whippet Club began in 2013; like The Whippet Club, it established a Racing Association to preserve the sporting talents of the purebred Whippet, as there were concerns over the loss of those valuable original breeding lines, and worries concerning the increase in the height of the Whippets taking part. The Sporting Whippet Club's criteria brought in restrictions to height in three categories: Whippets up to a height of 21in (54cm), standard males 18.5–20in (47–51cm), and standard females of 17.5–18.5in (44–47cm). As with the racing Whippets, a passport system confirmed their identity and acceptance. As in the coursing field, the Whippets are released by a slipper to run.

Lure coursing is also very popular in Europe; the rules are overseen by the Fédération Cynologique Internationale (FCI), and are different to those here in the UK. All dogs are licensed before they can run, and are required to pass trials for their capabilities to run cleanly without interfering with another dog. Many enthusiasts now travel to compete in FCI countries where lure-coursing championships are held, and it is possible to gain working titles. A newly formed UK Sighthound

The slipper, wearing traditional red, releasing Whippets at lure coursing.

Sport Club has recently worked to gain recognition by The Kennel Club for lure coursing to be registered here as a sport. This would mean that Whippets could be acknowledged as UK lure-coursing champions if they achieved three lure-coursing certificates (LCC). This sport truly does allow a Whippet to show how it is built for speed and work.

Unlike the racing Whippet, those that chase the lure need not be specifically bred for this sport, which is a great opportunity for any Whippet to have a go. However, there are breeders who have a reputation for their Whippets excelling at this sport. Here again, it is a case of attending a lure-coursing meeting and getting to know what happens, and making that connection with the experts.

CHAPTER 10

Obedience and Other Disciplines

Basic Obedience

In Chapter 5, basic training for your puppy was mentioned, and one way of teaching your Whippet to sit. You will have found that your Whippet loves to please, and is eager and quick to learn more. Obedience is the original discipline and the foundation that can lead to you being able to participate in other sports such as agility, flyball, heelwork to music, rally, and there are many others. It also contributes to a well behaved Whippet.

Here are some notes on training your Whippet from a very experienced judge and trainer, Pat Wilson:

> All puppies should start their training when they join your household. You will obviously be tackling house training, feeding and bedtime, so also start introducing your sit and down commands. Show the puppy what you want – don't just say 'sit, sit, sit' and expect your eight-week-old baby to understand. Show the puppy what you want, have a small, tasty titbit (not boring biscuits or chews but cheese, cooked liver, chicken, sausage – something tasty and smelling nice) and put the puppy into position followed by an instant 'good' and a titbit. You will be amazed at the number of people who give constant commands when the puppy doesn't yet understand and occasionally give boring titbits as a reward. Quality always if you want results! Your puppy probably already has a lightweight collar on so obviously short walks

Eager to learn and sit on command.

117

on a lead to introduce that element, initially in your garden, again using food to show the puppy what you want. Keep the food at puppy height (difficult I know with a small dog, but no pain no gain!) and at the end of their nose so they can follow at heel level.

Recall

Start recall training in the kitchen, living room or other confined space in your home, moving into the garden when you have got 100 per cent results inside. Don't even consider letting your puppy off the lead until it returns to you on command – if necessary, and if you are not sure, when eventually you go down to your local park, attach a sixteen feet or longer leash with a knot every couple of yards (for you to stand on and stop the puppy in its tracks) and let the puppy run with this on; initially you hold on to it until it gets used to it. As far as I am concerned, I consider that teaching recall, down, and sit on command is imperative, and then you

cannot go far wrong. However, the more you can teach your dog, even tricks, will improve their life considerably, and you are building a good relationship with your Whippet.

Training Class

If you decide to go to a dog-training class, I would want the puppy to be able to sit or lie down even for short periods. Research your local area – ask questions, and visit classes without your dog so that you can observe what is going on there without the distraction of your puppy. If you are not happy with what you see, then look elsewhere. If a class does not accept any dogs under, say, six months, then give it a wide berth. The bigger and older the dog, the more difficulty you will have in handling it.

The Kennel Club can give you details of anything in your area, but not all classes are KC registered. This doesn't mean don't touch them – they can be better! If you decide to join a class, then go armed with plenty of titbits, ask

Walking to heel during an obedience exercise – but this can be taught on everyday walks.

questions if you don't understand something, make sure you have comfortable, flat footwear on (heels and puppy feet don't mix) and hopefully enjoy spending time with your baby. If you go to a registered or affiliated class, you may find that they operate the Kennel Club Good Citizen assessments, bronze, silver and gold. All that adds to your dog's learning and hopefully your enjoyment.

Agility

This is one of the most enjoyable disciplines that Whippets can take part in, as they are using their ability to be quick moving and to turn on a sixpence, and are eager to please. It also exercises their brain and is fun, with

a great community of competitors. As with obedience, your Whippet will be required to have learnt some basics already, so attending your classes will help you progress. Your Whippet should be able to sit, stay and do recall confidently, but should also understand instructions for direction, maybe using a plant pot to walk around at home. As with obedience, tasty treats and toys are essential, and with practice your Whippet should soon understand what you are asking it to do.

Dogs are not allowed to compete until they are eighteen months old, so there is plenty of time to learn, and they are not allowed to practise jumping or high impact obstacles, so there is no danger of causing harm to young limbs. There are also contact obstacles such as tunnels, weaving poles, 'A' frames and seesaw, hoop, long jump and water jump. So you can see how much fun they could have. There is a large selection of agility-type equipment freely available now, so you can practise and have fun at home in the garden.

There are five different types of agility show, and these have specific criteria as you work through the different levels. There are seven different grades, starting at grade 1 for owners, handlers and dogs – dogs not to have gained a minimum of two grade 1 first places. So it is dependent on how far your Whippet takes you through these.

A nice close sit as the handler 'halts'.

Zigzagging between the poles.

Vinny clearing a jump.

Down the 'A' frame.

There is a height limit for dogs: in the large dog category dogs measure over 500mm at the withers (shoulder), intermediate dogs measure over 430mm up to 500mm, medium dogs are over 350mm and up to 430mm, and small dogs measure 350mm or under. So mostly Whippets will fit into the intermediate height limit. The course is designed by the judge on the day, so will be different every time; the time for completing the course is also set by the judge. This is a great sport for all ages of dog and handler – many Whippets have competed at the highest level and many go on into their more senior years and still enjoy taking part. It is even possible to take up agility later in your Whippet's life; it may not 'wish' to do some of the exercises, but will still learn some of them and that will extend its mobility, being a great form of exercise for both you and your Whippet.

Sarah Thomas specialises in agility along with her Whippet Vinny, and tells her story:

Vinyasa Blue Diamond is now seven years old; she started agility and flyball when she was twelve months old. She has always been very food motivated, so rewarding her training with food was a hit. We attended classes each week and slowly progressed to our first show in 2017 – by this time she was eighteen months old and could use all the equipment. She has always been a very confident dog, and doesn't have the nervous side that some whippets can have. She is from working lines and I believe her father is very outgoing. So the journey progressed with fun shows, and then we started UKA agility.

Vinny, as I call her, moved up the grades quickly from beginner to novice and on to senior, and achieved championship level by early 2019. This was in agility, jumping and games classes where you needed to obtain points to progress. We had also started Kennel Club agility, starting in grade 1 and we're heading up 2, 3, 4, 5. This was achieved by wins in agility and jumping. Vinny was jumping a low height of 55cm, but for qualifiers 65cm was the height, which was pretty high for my little whippet. We decided to chase the ABC qualifiers in 2019, where the dog can be anything but a collie – this helps other breeds have a chance to shine at shows such as Crufts.

We travelled around the country obtaining points, and managed to get enough to get to the semi-final at Discover Dogs in October 2019. Vinny had to jump 65cm on carpet against all the large breeds, and she coped very well. It was loud and noisy, but she's a natural show-off and came eighth overall. So we were competing at Crufts 2020 on the green carpet and with live television. Lots of practice took place in that time. It was two rounds again, agility and jumping, with a combined score. We had a clear round in the jumping, but sadly five faults in the agility so came fifth overall. But wow, what an experience.

Vinny is still competing, but I pick and choose her runs. She doesn't like extreme heat or rain or when it is too cold – after all, she is a whippet! But she will only do it for her sausage nosebag after her run, that's her reward. She is an absolute princess, my dog in a million. I have other successful agility dogs, but Vinyasa is where I started and I love running her – I hope she lives forever!

Heelwork To Music

If you have watched Crufts or some of the talent competitions on the television, you will probably have seen the talented dog and handlers performing their routines that are the 'Heelwork to Music' exercises. They are designed to show teamwork between the dog and handler in showing their skilful heelwork and freestyle movements in their interpretation of the music. It is always a great crowd pleaser and tearjerker! The Heelwork to Music exercises involve a larger part of the routine being actual walking to heel, whereas the Freestyle only allows one third of the routine to be heelwork. The exercises are at a set time limit, depending on which of the four levels you are working at. There is Starters up to 2½ minutes, up to Advanced at 4 minutes. The use of props and costumes is allowed, fitting in with the music's theme.

This is a very specialist type of training and needs a dedicated handler and much hard work; your Whippet would need to be a minimum of twelve months old to compete. The difference here is that the handler is part of the routine, unlike in some of the other disciplines, and there's a chance to dress up!

Sarah Thomas and Vinny work together round the course.

Flyball

Flyball was introduced to the UK in 1994, and the British Flyball Association was founded to regulate the sport and establish a grounding for rules and organising the sport. Since its inception, the Association has grown to be a tremendously popular sport with over 3,000 members involving 150,000 dogs and a membership of 450 teams, with competitions taking place all year round all over the country. The overriding appeal is that any breed can take part as long as they are eighteen months old. It is ideal for a Whippet as a way to maintain its fitness and keep it healthy; it is a rigorous sport of racing fun, which, of course, has great appeal to Whippets. For all ages in a family, there is plenty of socialising, friendship and team spirit. Teams are always looking for new members, so to get started there is intermediate and starter racing for dogs and handlers that are new to the sport. Note that you are not able to compete in these races until your Whippet is at least twelve months old.

In a competition two teams compete against each other. Each team consists of four dogs, with two reserves in addition. The competition is run over a 51ft long course, with handlers and dogs starting from behind a start line. The course is straight, with electronic timing sensors and lights that regulate each race line. The course has a series of jumps that are raised or lowered according to the size of the dogs being run. At the far end of the line is a box loader, who as well as loading the box with balls, encourages each dog from its handler as the race starts.

When the dog is released from its handler it runs down the course, clearing all the jumps, and at the end of the mat pushes the ball box with its front feet: this releases a ball, which it grabs and returns to its handler. This is, of course, all at breakneck speed – after all, it is a race! The opponent in the next lane is running simultaneously. The handlers must time the release of the next dog so that the finishing dog and the starting dog's noses cross the line at the same time. This continues until all four members of the team have run. The winners are declared by the judge.

The British Flyball Association has an excellent website where you can find out the nearest club to you, and what the sport is all about.

The first catch of the ball must be a secure one.

Pushing off from the baseboard.

The pasterns above the foot flex to cushion the impact on the baseboard.

The height of the jumps is adjusted to the size of the dog competing.

Whippets are fast compared to other breeds not known for their speed.

Taking the jumps in their stride.

CHAPTER **11**

The Art of Breeding

Good females are plentiful but it is difficult to find a good male.

Flavius Arrian

There are some important questions that need to be answered before you take the huge commitment as a breeder. To begin as a breeder, there are many things to consider. Why do you want to breed from your Whippet? You may feel it would be nice to have a puppy from your own Whippet for sentimental reasons. However, is it not possible to buy another related puppy from the same breeder? It is definitely not a money-making exercise if done properly, but an expensive and time-consuming undertaking. As a breeder, you have a lifetime of responsibility for all the puppies you breed, and not just for the first eight weeks of their life, because they must all be found a permanent, loving home.

In Chapter 5 a puppy contract was discussed, with the possibility that you made a breeding agreement with the breeder for using your male at stud or breeding from your female. If this is the case, it may be that you are bound by that arrangement. You need to know exactly what is expected of you. It may not be a good time for you when you are called upon to fulfil your commitment, or a few years down the line your circumstances may be such that it is not what you want to do. Think carefully.

Selective Breeding

Most experienced breeders are using their background knowledge of past generations, shown in the form of pedigrees and personal experience combined with an informed view of their own stock, before they commit to breeding a litter. The reason they are breeding a litter in the first place is usually because they would like to keep a puppy themselves to continue their line. One of the fundamental requirements is that a breeder knows their own stock inside out, and recognises the strong points, and more importantly the faults in their breeding stock. They may have stud dogs and brood bitches – those that are specifically used for breeding – which because of their bloodlines and their individual qualities are often kept with breeding in mind.

A successful line is dependent on the breeder choosing the right parents of the next litter to maximise the positive aspects, but also not to be 'kennel blind' and to recognise the faults within those lines. To establish a 'line'

Selective breeding brings the best qualities to the fore and reduces the chance of undesirable traits.

means that much expertise must be used, and this cannot be done in a hurry – that is, not in just a couple of generations. For many it is a lifetime achievement, and certainly if done properly, could be at least a ten-year project. In the past, many of the more famous and successful breeders kept a large number of one breed, and probably bred many litters from them – and you would think that by the law of averages they would produce a few top winners. In some cases that happened, but the objective of most dedicated breeders was, and still should be, to produce a line that is strong in breed type as well as being recognisable as showing a breeder's type.

As mentioned earlier, when breed type and type within a breed was discussed, it is important to build on the breed's characteristics and add quality and consistency, not only to just a few dogs, but to generations of the same bloodline so it becomes recognisable as a breeder's own type.

Line Breeding

Breeders studying pedigrees are looking for similarities in the bloodlines, which can often be in close relatives, in order to bring together and practise line breeding. This can standardise the offspring to have a family resemblance. At the same time, a breeder's knowledge of the pedigree of past dogs will tell them what the offspring of those individual dogs were like and if they passed on their positive traits – but it also warns them of faults that occurred, whether that was in just one litter or consistently. Many breeders will look at males that may be suitable for breeding, and if they are attracted by their looks, will then research their bloodlines with those criteria in mind.

Line breeding is the bringing together of two distantly related lines that share common ancestry from the third generation back. There may also be a few lines of totally

Line breeding uses similar lines to produce puppies with a family resemblance.

unrelated dogs in the pedigree: the important thing here is that the lines do not carry any breed faults that you would not want to introduce into your line. Equally, you do not want to introduce another line that carries a fault that you already have, because you will be doubling up on a breed fault that will make it almost impossible to eradicate in the future.

Close Breeding

Close breeding is similar to line breeding, but the pedigree is mostly made up of closely related dogs; it was practised by many successful breeders. It is now regarded as unethical to carry out such matings as brother to sister, mother to son, but better to remain with a more open co-efficient of inbreeding. The object of close breeding was to reduce the number of different lines and thus concentrate the bloodlines, removing any traits that were undesirable. The results of such breeding established a breeder's type very quickly. The negative result was that this kind of breeding often brought out any breed faults, if they were indeed present in the bloodlines. This highlighted to the breeder what they had to breed away from.

The crux of this type of breeding was that the breeder had to recognise at what point they had to bring in fresh blood to strengthen their lines to prevent losing a certain degree of robustness. Finding an outcross for such a strong type was very difficult. Two strong types tended not to complement each other in breeder's type, and split litters of not very good quality were often the result. The breeder's talent in knowing instinctively how to progress was the difference between success and failure. In the past many successful breeders used this type of breeding, which in turn had a strong influence on the way the breed developed. These stud dogs were usually popular because they consistently produced champions.

Outcrossing

Many breeders use the outcrossing method of breeding on a regular basis. The simple criterion of choosing a male because he looks appealing or because he runs the fastest can be all that is needed, and the resulting litter may have the attributes desired. The long-term problem may be that by introducing dogs that are unrelated to one another every time, the bloodlines are diluted so much that the resulting puppies begin to lose breed type. On the other hand, introducing a complete outcross to a line or closely bred Whippet can reinvigorate that line.

The important factor here is the breeder uses their knowledge and instincts to balance out the possibilities that may appear in that litter. If they are satisfied with the resulting offspring, they can then carefully select future breeding stock to progress to the next generation when

Two typical heads, showing essential breed points.

these are put back to their own lines. A breeder should be mindful of the Whippet's future as a breed. In the mid-sixties and onwards into the 1990s there was a strong nucleus of dominant stud dogs that produced consistently, and their influence can be seen in pedigrees today.

Colour Breeding

Colour breeding may seem an odd subject to be discussing, as the Whippet can be any colour or combination of colours. However, the term 'colour breeding' specifically relates to the breeding of blacks and blues. In the dominance of coat colours black is a dominant colour, and can linger in a pedigree and surprise the most experienced breeder when a black puppy appears in an otherwise more commonly coloured litter. Colour breeding for blacks and blues adds an extra consideration to the breeder's choice of stud dog or brood bitch. These two colours are notoriously hard to breed whilst at the same time producing a good quality Whippet. Latterly the problems were mainly that the litter lacked bone substance and good shape, but a few dedicated breeders have taken up the challenge and produced very lovely blacks and blues, and there have been champions in the show ring.

These two colours are also very popular within racing circles, as blacks are known to have a good turn of speed. Coat-colour inheritance is a very complicated subject, especially when there are so many choices of colour – but very basically the dominance order is black, brindle, fawn and white. Blue is not mentioned in this order as it is a recessive colour of black, not to mention the creams in the lighter colours.

But to concentrate on blacks and blues, because black is the dominant colour it can cover all the other colours – the only way it will be in the minority is if it is not a dominant black. This means that it is a product of a mixed combination of colours that carry black, but are not a pure colour. This can be seen by shading of the coat in a black, often as much as a rusty red tinge to the coat. To establish if your male is a dominant black he needs to be bred to a variety of different colours, and the resulting puppies should be mainly black. So black to black and black to blue, if pure, should produce black and a few blue puppies. These blue puppies will not produce black unless they are put to another black, as blue is recessive.

Colour breeding normally means breeding black Whippets, seen here with white trim.

Lovely quality blacks are very stylish, but can be difficult to breed.

If you mated a dominant black to a brindle, you will get black puppies in the litter, providing the stripes on the brindle bitch are black or it has a black mask. If the stripes or mask is blue you will get blue puppies.

In theory, even if your Whippet has one single black hair it will produce black when put to a dominant black; the problem is that sometimes it doesn't show in the resulting puppies, but it is still lurking behind them, and can come out at any stage many generations into the future. The subject is very complex because of the large number of colour variations, but these are the basic principles.

Breeding from your Male Whippet

As a stud-dog owner your responsibility is to ensure that the resulting puppies of any mating, including those being brought into the world by another breeder, are well bred, healthy, and reared correctly in suitable surroundings. Firstly, if the opportunity to breed from your male Whippet arises, you may need to check any agreement you may have entered into with your own dog's breeder when you bought him as a puppy, as to whether he would be available to be used at stud. This might be for one litter, or multiple litters throughout his life, and with this agreement in place there should be no doubt as to the understanding between you and the breeder. The stud fees should be agreed on, and who will get the stud fee. It may be for his breeder's own use only, in which case there will be no stud fee, or for others to come and use him at stud where a stud fee would be required. Do you want this as an ongoing occurrence? It could be at an inconvenient time (and usually is!), and are you prepared to travel to the breeder's home for the mating to take place?

There is also the possibility that your pet will become unsettled by being used at stud. It will stimulate your Whippet's inner feelings, and subsequently he will always be aware of bitches around him and while out exercising, which he may not have been bothered about until that time. These seem very negative points but in reality it can be a problem, the implications of which you may not be aware of.

If there is no such agreement you are not obliged to comply with the breeder's wishes; however, your dog's breeder may not be too happy about him being used at stud by someone else in the first place. The reasons behind this are that he was probably sold to you as a pet, and may not have the qualities that a stud dog should possess on a number of points. Remember, a good breeder should always have the preservation of the breed uppermost in their mind. If you are approached by another owner, unconnected to the breeder, ask them why they wish to use your dog, and ask if their female has a pedigree and is Kennel Club registered. It may be that the bitch's owner would like to incorporate your dog's bloodlines with their own.

Remember that the breeder of your Whippet has nurtured their lines possibly for many years, and may feel that this female is not suitable for a number of reasons, so always seek advice from them. The owner of the female may just like the way your dog looks, and although this is a traditional way of choosing a stud dog, it is not a strong enough reason to allow him to be used. If she has a pedigree, the offspring should be purebred and of a type. If the female has no pedigree, her ancestors may be of other origins and the resulting litter may be mixed and not purebred. In any case, if you are not sure, it is always wise to contact your Whippet's breeder and seek their experienced opinion.

It is usual practice for the owner of the female to pay a stud fee to the dog's owner at the time of mating. This stud fee is normally representative of the price of buying a puppy, but this should be decided on well in advance with the involved parties. If there are no puppies born as a result of the mating, a future mating could be offered to the bitch's owner. This can be a problem, and it should be established why the bitch did not produce puppies from the previous mating. The following points should be considered: first, are both your dog and the bitch fertile? Might it be possible one of them has a problem, such as a virus that is preventing them from conceiving? It is better to establish these facts, for peace of mind. However, it should be noted that some dogs never produce puppies, for no apparent reason.

As the stud dog owner you will be required to complete and sign a portion of a Kennel Club registration application form: you should sign this when the puppies have arrived. You may decide to agree to have a puppy from the litter in lieu of the stud fee, but this is at the discretion of the female's owner, who may prefer to pay the stud fee. How to manage a stud dog at the time of mating is discussed later.

Breeding from your Female Whippet

Many of the initial questions outlined above are still relevant. Why do you want to breed from your female Whippet? Most owners would love to have another Whippet (one is never enough!), especially from their own Whippet, but this is often a decision made by the heart rather than the head. The old saying, 'She needs to have one litter before she is spayed' really is just that – an old saying. Owning a bitch means that she will regularly come into season around every six months or so, and at this time she will show a discharge for around three weeks, during which time she will be receptive to males. This discharge is mainly blood – the quantity varies, but it can be quite messy around the house. There are dog sanitary products available to help with this. Also she should not be taken out in public places during this time, as an interesting scent will be left every time she wees, which will attract unwanted interest from male dogs.

The season lasts for a period of three weeks on average, and during the middle part of this period the bitch is usually at her most fertile. The discharge at this point will change to a clear fluid; by the end of the three weeks she will return to normal. If you choose to have your female spayed, this will remove her ability to come into season, and you will not be able to breed a litter from her; this is perfect for a pet. A word of caution: following being spayed you should be aware that she will put on weight quite easily, so strict food management is important. Contact your vet for advice on the process, as they will need to establish when your female is in mid-cycle as the blood supply to that area is lower than around her season time. Make an appointment to have her spayed when you can spend time with her during recovery after the operation.

Any breeding should be from a quality stud dog and brood bitch. A pair that have similar lines and look similar are a good start.

Deciding on Having a Litter

A decision has been made! You would like to breed from your female. As discussed earlier, this may be part of an agreement made with your Whippet's breeder, and often to maximise the quality of your puppies, the breeder may already have a suitable stud dog in mind. Either way, it would be courtesy to discuss this with them, and to get an opinion on what dog would be suitable. There are many dogs available and it is usual to contact the owner of a stud dog in plenty of time before the bitch is due in season to ask if he would be available to your female. A responsible stud-dog owner will ask about her parentage and may wish to see her. It may be that they will not allow him to be used, but that is their prerogative, and you should respect this without being offended. If, however, they are happy for you to use him, you must ask how much the stud fee is and be prepared to pay this at the time of mating.

It is normal practice not to breed from your bitch before she is eighteen months old, or until she has had at least two seasons, and definitely not on her first season, when she could well still be a puppy herself. Waiting until she is at least eighteen months old enables your Whippet to be in prime condition and fully matured, whilst still being supple enough to produce puppies. If your bitch is older, for instance five or six years old, and has never had puppies before, then it is unwise to breed from her, as it may cause problems when she is due to whelp the puppies. If your bitch is unable to whelp the puppies naturally, be prepared that she will need a Caesarean section: this can be very costly, and most veterinary practices expect payment before they do the operation.

Preparing for the Mating

You have now arranged which stud dog you are going to use, and your Whippet bitch is due to come into season. As mentioned earlier, she can come into season

Similarly bred Whippets can still have individual differences.

on average every six months, although this is not set in stone. Sometimes a first season can be at around six months of age, but this is unusually early, and normally it would be any time from eleven to around eighteen months; all are quite normal as it is an individual thing, as are the days that she will be ready to be served by the dog. It is unethical to breed from your Whippet before she is eighteen months old, as already outlined, so a good time is around this age, as long as she has had one season before this date.

You should contact the stud-dog owner as soon as possible to inform them that she is in season, and that you will be going ahead. It is customary for you to travel to the stud dog. Do not leave it until the day before she is ready for mating. Many people often ask about using a dog at stud but never get back in touch, so confirm your intentions, giving plenty of time for arrangements to be made for everyone.

As your bitch comes into season she will start to lose drops of blood from her vulva; this can be quite profuse, or may be just the occasional drop. As the season progresses her vulva will begin to enlarge, and the blood flow can increase. It is usual to count the days from the first time you see drops of blood, as your bitch will be at her most fertile in mid-cycle. The peak of being 'ready' can be from ten to fourteen days, but again this is not set in stone. To take the guesswork out of estimating her peak, there are blood tests your vet can do that would indicate the time of maximum fertility, giving you about twenty-four hours warning. To try and estimate when to take the blood test, the blood from your bitch's vulva will start to change to a clear discharge and she will be very 'flirty'. This flirtiness is shown by her flying her tail from side to side and presenting her rear to other dogs.

The Day of Mating

Your Stud Dog
Your male Whippet is about to be used at stud, and it is important that if you are inexperienced, you call on a person who knows what to do and help, as it is very

Pauline Oliver with a winning brace of well-matched girls.

much 'hands on'. Do not allow your Whippet any food for a couple of hours before the mating as he will probably bring it all back up during the mating process when he gets excited. When the bitch arrives at the appointed time, you need to go to a space where the floor is washable, fairly comfortable to sit on, and in private. It would be inappropriate if the vicar called in the middle of the mating on your front doorstep!

The owner is normally in charge of holding the bitch at her front throughout the mating process: this prevents her snapping at the dog and helps to keep her reasonably still. When your male comes to the bitch, he will flirt with her, and she in turn should flirt with him. He will then try to mount her, which she may object to at the start, and this is when the owner must hold the bitch firmly. The dog should then enter the bitch, but an inexperienced dog may take a few attempts to do so, and he may need a rest period as he will get quite hot and flustered. When he actually succeeds and enters the bitch, they will 'tie':

they will be held together for a period of time, which can last anything from ten to forty-five minutes. When the mating is over, the dog will withdraw and he is taken from the room. It is important you take him away and allow him to cool down and settle. After the mating, take note that the sheath around his penis returns to normal.

Taking your Bitch for Mating

You should ensure that your Whippet is as calm as possible, and if you are travelling a long distance, bear this in mind. On arrival at the stud-dog owner's premises, leave her in the car and announce your arrival. If it is your first time being present at a mating, tell the owner this, and ask what they wish you to do. You will be directed to where the mating will take place with your bitch; keep her secured on her collar and lead. When the dog arrives, she may be upset and try to snap at the dog initially: this is normal. The dog will often try to play with her and flirt with her – she may return the compliment, or may not be that impressed!

Hopefully after a short time she will be more amenable to him. If not, the stud-dog owner may suggest putting a muzzle on her to prevent any injuries if she continues to snap – they will probably have one available.

The dog will mount the bitch and start to enter her; this may take a few attempts but eventually he will succeed and they will 'tie'. They will then be tied together for anything from ten to forty-five minutes, as said above. At this time it is imperative that they are kept still by holding them closely together, either both facing the same way, or often a stud dog will turn and face the opposite way. If they are allowed to move excessively there is a chance of causing injury to the stud dog. It is the bitch that is holding the dog inside her, and at the end of the mating she will release him and he will withdraw. The stud-dog's owner will then take him away.

You should keep your bitch quiet and put her in the car for a short while before you leave. The stud-dog's owner could suggest you may have another mating either the next day or the day after that. This is customary, but entirely your choice – some believe that just one good mating is sufficient. If your bitch has not been successfully mated, you should discuss this with the stud-dog's owner, and they may suggest another day if in their experience she may not have been quite ready. This can often be the case, despite all the signs, and a successful mating could be achieved a few days later. Remember, this is a natural process and sometimes it simply doesn't happen.

There are occasions when the stud dog will not perform, and if his owner has another dog available this may be an option for you; however, as he isn't the dog of your choice, be aware that he may not be as suitable as your first choice, and you are making a snap decision, not the considered one you made some time before.

Slip Matings

There is a possibility that during the above process the dog and bitch do not tie. In this case the dog may enter the bitch as described above, but she fails to hold the dog inside her. If this happens a few times, it is possible that the bitch is not at her peak for mating. This is a good reason to use the fertility test done by your vet, as it eliminates this from the possibilities. It may also be that the male only performs slip matings, which is uncommon but not unknown. This doesn't necessarily mean he won't sire any puppies, but it can be overcome by good handling.

The best thing to do when the male enters the bitch is to push with the flat of your hand on his rump, so that he is held in position. You can stimulate the male by manipulating the large, swollen bulb-type area on his penis. Hold the two together for as long as possible. When they do part, lift the bitch's hindquarters to keep any fluids inside her for a few minutes. This is not foolproof but is worth a try. Often it is the case that the bitch is either not ready to be mated, or she has already passed the fertile period. Either way, you should still keep a close eye on her in case she is in whelp to this slip mating.

Caring For The Expectant Mum

It is very much a waiting game after the mating for nine weeks until the puppies arrive; you may not see any signs that your bitch is in whelp in the early days, though sometimes she will go off her food and may be sick a few times. This is similar to morning sickness experienced by us, and she will soon be back to normal. It is important that you regulate her food whilst she is pregnant. Feed a good balanced diet of normal portions to begin with, but in the later stages of her pregnancy you will need to increase the quantity of food as she starts to draw on her own reserves to feed the growing puppies inside her. At this stage it may be better to split her feed into smaller portions, and rather than two big meals in the day, feed these for example four times in the day, as her distended abdomen makes it difficult for her to cope with a larger meal.

For the first four weeks you probably won't see any changes in the bitch's physique, but at five weeks into the pregnancy she will be starting to lose her tuck-up and her tummy will begin to grow rounder. Now is the time that your vet can scan her to estimate the number of puppies she will be having. A Whippet is shaped such that she can carry puppies high up in her ribcage, and often there are no tell-tale signs that she is in whelp at all, so a scan is useful for this. However, the vet can only give a rough idea of the number of puppies by listening for heartbeats: often puppies lie side by side and are hidden from the scanner, so don't take the number as certain. A scan is really more to confirm whether she is in whelp or not.

If there are no puppies visible she probably isn't in whelp, but it is advisable to keep an eye on her a few days past her due date just in case. This can be caused by a number of reasons. Perhaps the stud dog is infertile, although if he has been used before it is unlikely. Your bitch may be infertile, though again this is rare when she has regular, normal seasons. The day(s) she was mated was (were) not when she was ovulating at her peak: she may be a bitch that ovulates earlier or later than the mid cycle and she wasn't ready for mating, or the peak had passed.

There is also the possibility that perhaps she has an infection, which has not been evident until now. If this is the case, with treatment she should go on to produce puppies normally next time, but it is important to ask your vet for their advice. If this is the case it is best to treat it straightaway so there is no risk of the infection spreading or getting worse, and to be sure it is cleared up well in advance of next time. Out of courtesy you should inform the stud-dog owner that this has happened, as the stud dog may also need treatment.

What You will Need for the Nursery

If your Whippet is clearly in whelp, it is never too soon to get organised. You need to think where you will keep the puppies when they are born, and the equipment and space that you will need to rear the litter. At the time of birth, the puppies need to be warm, with plenty of light for the bitch so she can see what is happening, so a suitable room that is quiet and warm is ideal. The floor and walls should be washable as the birthing fluid can be quite profuse and uncontrollable. A suitable bed or box to have the puppies in also needs to be washable or disposable after the puppies have moved out.

There are excellent birthing or whelping boxes on the market. Some are quite expensive as they are an insulated plastic-type bed and will last for a long time, not just one litter, or there are more cost-effective disposable cardboard boxes designed for puppies in mind. The whelping box should be a good size so there is room for both puppies and mum to move around and lie comfortably. As the puppies grow there should be plenty of room for everyone. The box should have high sides to prevent draughts, and the front should have a removable panel to allow mum to come out, and later for small puppies to come out and get back in when they are older and more mobile. Ideally a suitable box would measure 76cm wide × 115cm long × 60–80cm high. These boxes vary in price and can be costly, depending on the quality of the box.

If you are having the box sited in a room in your house, the central heating will probably keep them warm enough. If you choose to have the puppies in an outbuilding or kennel outside, this should be free from draughts, and it will be necessary to install an infra-red heat lamp or some sort of safe heating. Heat lamps provide a good heat source to ensure the puppies dry off quickly once they are born, and that they remain warm. There are electric heat pads available that are also good, but it is important that you monitor that the puppies are comfortable, as they can get too hot and may be unable to move away from the heat source.

Once the puppies are mobile, they will need an area to run around in until they can go outside in the garden. As your litter grows they will need more space, but they will also need to be contained within that area. Pet playpens made up of sectional panels are suitable for this, but make sure the playpen is high enough to prevent the puppies climbing out when they get bigger. There should be a door in one of the panels for you to step in and out of the pen.

It is a good idea to start saving old newspapers, as these are absolutely essential. The whelping box can be lined with newspaper on the base to soak up any birthing fluids; this should be changed often, at least twice a day in the early days. On top of the newspapers, an absorbent fleece-type bedding is ideal; it can be bought from good pet suppliers. It allows the fluids to pass through whilst keeping the upper part dry, and is machine washable. Again, this should be changed often, so it is a good idea to have two or three fleeces that can be changed while the others are being washed. This type of bedding wears well and dries very quickly after washing. Newspapers can also be used on the floor to allow the puppies, as they grow, to come out of the box to clean themselves. They will soon understand that the newspaper is where they go to do their toilet, and is the first stage of house training.

Looking Ahead

When the puppies are around four weeks old, they will need a space where they can run around and play, as well as fresh air. Puppies born in the winter time should only be allowed out for a short period, weather permitting, as they will quickly get a chill. They will also be harder to keep clean as they carry mud and moisture inside on their paws. So it is important that indoors they have plenty of room. In the summertime it is much easier to have puppies running around in the warm sunshine. They should have access to water at all times, and there should be suitable shade as the sun moves round during the day.

With just a few weeks to go, the expectant mum has a full, rounded tummy and has lost her tuck-up.

Whatever the season, the puppies should have their bed inside where they can retire to sleep during the day.

So as you can see, there is quite a lot to buy and arrange before the puppies are born. This should all be decided on, set up and ready a minimum of one week before they are due. During this time your Whippet can be a part of the preparations, and you should allow her to investigate it all. She will then be familiar with the box and will be happy to have her puppies there. A bitch often decides that the best place to have her puppies is in an extremely inaccessible hole in the garden! However, she will soon settle in the whelping box once the puppies start to arrive.

Preparing for the Puppies' Arrival

There are a few supplies you can buy in readiness. A feeding regime is discussed later, but stocking up in advance is a good plan. Goat's milk is a good product for both the bitch after she has whelped and the puppies later, once they are weaned. It is available from goat breeders, or now in most supermarkets; its great advantage is that it can be frozen and stored until needed.

There is a multitude of puppy foods available, from tinned meat to dry, complete feeds specially produced for both mother and baby. It is a matter of choice and depth of pocket, but a brand that offers food for each stage of the puppies' growth and their breed size will give them the best start. Some brands make a mousse that is designed for weaning puppies; it is available in small tins, ideal portions that eliminate waste.

A selection of dishes is a good idea, some for the first tastes of food – for example a large saucer or pie plate, where the sides are not too high for reaching into. The puppies will soon progress to a larger dish, big enough for all the litter to gather round it at the same time. A deeper dish for water should be of a good weight as puppies tend to paddle in it and anything light can be easily tipped over.

Ten Days to Go

It is a good idea to contact your vet and let them know that your Whippet is due to whelp. This alerts them in case they are needed in an emergency. It is also the time to have the whelping box ready. It is surprising how quickly time goes and soon it is the due date for the puppies to arrive. Your Whippet will now be finding it more difficult to do the things she is used to, such as long walks, so let her decide what she feels is enough. During the last week or so her body will start to change and you can get an indication of how much nearer she is to the birthing day. By now she will have developed a large tummy, her teats will have enlarged, and her vulva will begin to enlarge and look more open. Your puppies could arrive at any time from now on, so it is important to keep a close eye on her.

She will have become increasingly hungry, but she doesn't have a lot of room to eat big meals with the puppies inside, so keep them little and often. She may occasionally start to lose a little clear jelly from her vulva: this is normal, and if the discharge changes colour or becomes profuse she may be starting to whelp. You can start to look out for further signs that she is nearing whelping. For example in the last week her tummy will 'drop', and you will see that her backbone is more prominent – there will be a hollow either side of it, as the puppies seem to be held lower in her tummy. As she gets nearer to whelping time, her tummy area will again tighten and become quite firm, and you can possibly see the puppies moving inside her body through her skin. She is making ready for their arrival.

The Puppies Start to Arrive

As your Whippet makes ready to whelp, she will become unsettled and will start to 'nest'. She will scratch at the bedding and try to build a nest, which really looks more like an uncomfortable heap! This can go on for quite a while but it is a sure sign that she will soon give birth. As the contractions start, she will start to pant, and then will soon start to strain with each contraction. How long this takes varies with each bitch, but you should keep a close eye on her. Take her outside to clean herself but preferably on the lead – this is an opportunity for her to disappear into that inaccessible hole! The puppies are now starting to move forwards down the birth canal. As each contraction gets stronger there will be a discharge from her, which may be dark green in colour. This discharge is normal and increases as the puppy gets nearer.

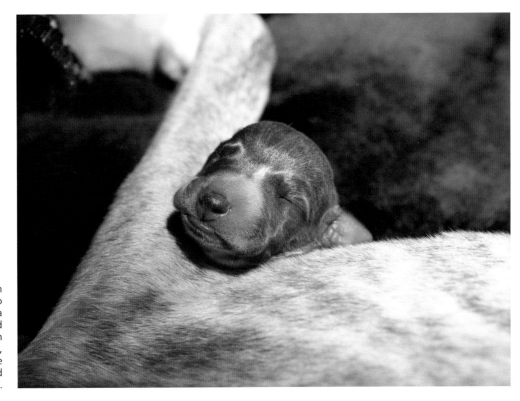

The newborn soon begins to dry and has a pink nose and feet. After a turn at the milk bar, the puppy will be very quiet and contented.

The first puppy can sometimes take quite a while to come out, but soon you will start to see a large 'bubble' of fluid and as it is passed out of the canal you can see the puppy inside. This is the sack that has protected the puppy during the gestation period. Hopefully you will begin to see the head and front legs of the puppy. If you can see two hind feet and a tail, the puppy is breach – that is, coming backwards. This bubble may burst and the fluid from it will gush out exposing the puppy.

Once the puppy has partially emerged with its head and forelegs showing, you can start to gently pull it out in unison with the mother's contractions. The puppy will be very wet and slippery, so an old clean towel could be used to help get hold of it firmly. Note that the puppy should normally be able to be born on its own without your help: it is for you to decide if you wish to assist and help it out. It is important to note that the puppy will come out in a downward direction, not straight out, and the first born can sometimes be a shade larger than the other puppies.

Once the puppy is born, it will still be attached to an afterbirth by the umbilical cord. The cord can be cut with a sharp pair of scissors, or the bitch will chew it and break it herself. You can give the puppy a gentle rub with your towel to ensure it is breathing, but should allow the bitch to begin to clean it herself. The puppy should squeak very quickly once it is stimulated; if it is slow and its nose doesn't start to turn pink, give it another good rub with the towel to encourage it to take a gasp and breathe. Your bitch will then take over licking the puppy to clean it, and very soon it will start to dry off and get warm.

Following each puppy is its own afterbirth; the bitch may well eat this, or you can remove it wrapped in a sheet of newspaper to dispose of later. In the event of a puppy

A waterproof whelping bed can be made from many things – here, it is a plastic paddling pool.

Nest of sleeping puppies. These are all brindle in colour.

A cage can also be used for puppies, here around two weeks old.

coming backwards, this breach birth is no different, and exactly the same applies; but often the bubble sack is already broken and you will see two hindlegs and a tail. Once these are exposed, you should wait until more of the puppy's body has been delivered before gently pulling it out with your towel – or again, allow the bitch to push the puppy out naturally.

If all goes well your puppies will arrive safely. They should come regularly, following short periods of contractions in between puppies. The puppies will have been in two 'horns' of the uterus, so it is usual that when one horn is emptied, there will be a gap in time before the puppies from the next horn begin to arrive. Your Whippet will take this interlude to have a sleep and a drink of milk or water, or you could take her out to clean herself at this point (on the lead). The next batch of puppies will start to come, and when she has finally had all the puppies she will fall into a deep sleep.

The puppies should dry off quickly as the mother will lick them clean of the birthing fluid. They will make a beeline for her teats, and very quickly will begin to feed; they should be settled and quiet, all with pink noses and feet, and soon their tummies will be round and full. When the puppies are settled, their mother will be too, but she may get anxious and agitated if a puppy is squeaking, especially in the first few days. This is her natural mothering instinct coming into play.

A puppy that is continually squeaky should be watched to make sure there is not a problem, such as a birth defect, or that it is getting enough milk from mum. Your bitch should begin to let her milk down after a day or so. There may be one puppy that is smaller than the others, which continually gets pushed out of the way as the stronger puppies feed. Spend time watching your puppies and you will quickly notice any problems. You can help them get a good drink of milk by placing them on the teat and making sure they get latched on.

Your Whippet will very quickly settle into her new role, and will want to eat as soon as she has finished whelping. With plenty of good food and drink she should produce adequate milk to provide for her new litter. As mentioned earlier, there are mother and baby dog foods on the market, and goat's milk is a good supplement for her; she should always have plenty of water available to drink.

The new family will grow quickly, and the puppies should be quiet, settled and warm. Your Whippet will look very bedraggled and thin immediately after having the puppies, but she will start to recover over the next couple of weeks, and begin to get her normal shape back. It is important to make sure that she is regularly taken out to clean herself, as she may be quite reluctant to leave her babies. She should settle down into a routine for the next two or three weeks as she nurses the puppies. The discharge from her will continue for quite a few weeks afterwards, but by the time the puppies are ten days old she should have dried up fairly well with only an occasional discharge. She should also have gained more body weight and look more like her old self.

With any new birth sometimes there may be a problem with a puppy; it is a natural process and it is not unusual for a puppy not to survive the birth process for whatever reason. Occasionally a birth defect can emerge, and as hard as it may be, you should be aware that this can happen and should be prepared to cope with this eventuality. In many cases the puppy may not survive, or it may need to be euthanased.

Caesarian Section

If the puppies do not start to be born despite the bitch having contractions and pushing for a while you should consult your vet if you feel it has gone on too long with still no puppies. Your bitch will quickly become distressed and look unhappy, and there may be a discharge from her. *This is an emergency* and if you do not seek the help of your vet you are endangering the lives of the puppies and your Whippet. The vet may advise she has a Caesarean section to deliver the puppies. You may be able to help the vet when the puppies are being delivered; help is often appreciated to get the puppies breathing by rubbing them with a towel. They will have taken some of the anaesthetic given to your Whippet, and can be a little slow in starting to breathe and squeak.

The newborns will need to be put to one side once they are revived, and placed in a cardboard box or pet carrier. The box should have a hot water bottle wrapped up in a towel in the base and a fleece blanket or towels on top of that. The blanket should be folded over so the puppies can be covered to retain the heat. Once all the puppies are born and settled, they can be taken home with mum.

Aftercare of your bitch is very important, as she will understandably be dozy from the anaesthetic. She will not be quite sure where the puppies have come from, especially if this is her first litter, so keep a close eye on her. Introduce the puppies to her by placing them, one by one, to her teats, where hopefully they will start to suckle

Finding a foster mother is a godsend. This mum took on a litter of Boston terriers as well as rearing her own puppies, which can be seen on the far left.

and she will accept them by starting to lick them clean. She may accept the puppies straightaway – or she may not accept them at all and will be aggressive towards them. If she growls, remove the puppies and you can repeatedly introduce the puppies one by one and hopefully she will begin to wash them and eventually accept them as her own. If she is unsure, never leave her unattended with the puppies as she may attack them. Fortunately Whippets are usually very good mothers, and you will have no problems introducing her to her puppies.

In rare cases, however, she may not accept them at all and you should move the puppies away. You will then have to decide if you are going to hold your bitch down while the puppies feed and remove them every time, which can be every two hours to start with. This is not only time consuming, but not the best situation for your bitch. She also may not produce any milk for the puppies. Finding a foster mum is probably the best option, but it is extremely lucky if you can find a bitch to take on your puppies just at the right stage. Of course this is

also dependent on the foster mother accepting the puppies. The worst-case scenario, and by far the most labour intensive, is to hand rear the puppies yourself.

Foster Mum or Hand Rearing

If you find yourself in this unenviable position, by far the best option is to try and find a foster mother. This is definitely achievable, and many litters have been saved by the mothering instinct of the most unlikeliest of breeds. Some bitches that have already reared their own puppies will come back into milk for more puppies, while others that have lost their own litter have been known to take on a surrogate litter. The main thing is that your puppies can get the right type of milk to survive, thrive and grow. You may have the foster mother and puppies, or the puppies could go to the mother: this is an agreement to be made between owners. You would normally take your puppies back around the time they have been weaned.

The decision to hand rear your puppies may be made for you. This is one of the most time-consuming jobs and

Mum will protect her puppies by lowering her head over them.

requires the puppies to be fed every two hours for at least the first week. You will need some equipment and hand-rearing kits are available, but essentially you need a feeding bottle with teats small enough to fit into the puppies' mouths. Formulated milk is available at good pet stores, and as with any babies, all equipment should be kept very clean, so use the proprietary baby feeding-bottle sterilising solutions.

The puppies can live in their pet carrier box for the first week or so, as it replicates the womb by being cosy and warm, and the puppies are bunched together. After this time, they could probably move to the original whelping box you had prepared, with the addition of extra heating if required. This is because they are not able to take the heat from their mother's body. The most important thing is that they are warm, dry and well fed. If you are looking after them properly, the puppies will be quiet and settled.

You are replicating their mother, and as well as feeding them, you need to clean the puppies after every feed. To do this, take a small piece of cotton wool moistened in warm water, wipe over the puppies' tummy and down under their tail, imitating how a bitch would clean them. This will stimulate them to clean themselves. Once clean, dry them with some kitchen towel, and rub a small dot of nappy cream or a similar barrier cream to prevent urine scalds on their thin skin. The puppies will be more soiled than normal, because usually the bitch tidies up after them constantly in their bed; therefore attention should be paid to the cleanliness of their bedding, which will need to be changed more often than if she was with them.

As the weeks go by and the puppies grow stronger they will take more feed and be satisfied for longer periods, but for the first two weeks tending for them is a very tiring vigil. The litter will probably take to weaning a little earlier than those with a mother present. It is useful for your own information and peace of mind to formulate a chart to follow each puppy's progress by weight gain.

Visitors

People are always excited to see new puppies, and everyone will want to visit. However, it is advisable not to allow visitors to begin with. When the puppies are born, your Whippet will naturally want to protect her babies, and even though normally she may be calm and friendly towards anyone, this is different, and she may become quite aggressive if she feels threatened. You might find this quite alarming, but she is only doing her job, and her feelings should be respected. Even when *you* go in, you may notice the hair on her back standing up: this indicates she is displeased, but will accept you under sufferance. There is always the risk that she will become unsettled, which makes the puppies squeak, which in turn makes her anxious.

As the puppies grow older her reaction will not be as intense, but always be aware that she may still wish to protect them, and especially from strangers. Children would love to get in the box with the puppies and stroke them, but this is strictly off limits; even when the puppies are older, children should only be allowed with the puppies under strict supervision, and never with the bitch present.

Another aspect is hygiene, in that any visitors may bring in an unwanted virus on their hands, clothes or shoes, which may affect the puppies adversely. Prospective puppy buyers can visit once the litter is around five weeks old, but their mum should be kept away from the puppy area as she may still be protective towards strangers. Ensure that these visitors wash their hands before and after touching the puppies. However, it is important to make sure the puppies are socialised and their personalities are developed by interaction with you and your close family. If the puppy box is situated in your home, it may be that they will experience all kinds of sights and sounds; if, however, they are in a quieter place, a radio playing gives them a variety of sounds when you are not there.

CHAPTER **12**

Rearing a Litter

Puppy Milestones

As the puppies grow in their first two to three weeks, they become increasingly active and their demands on mum become much greater. With good food, your bitch should manage to maintain a balance between feeding her puppies and maintaining her own bodyweight, having recovered from the actual births. You will notice that she may start to lose a little weight and will be increasingly hungry as the puppies' demands become more intense, so you should increase her meals and maybe feed her three times a day to maintain this balance.

The puppies in the nest will quickly develop from being helpless, blind things that crawl around in search of the warm heap of their siblings or to the comfort of their mum. The speed at which puppies change as they grow is always amazing, and by the time they are around two weeks old they will be up on their legs and starting to take unsteady steps. At the same time, or shortly after, their eyes begin to open. First you will see a faint glimmer in the inside corner of their eyes, and after a couple of days their eyes will be fully open. They are suddenly proper little Whippets!

Weaning The Puppies

When the puppies are around this age, have their eyes open and are starting to walk around, weaning can begin. There is no strict rule when this should happen, as often their mum is still providing plenty of milk for them and

they can remain well satisfied – but there is a point where their demands far outweigh what she can provide, and it is time to offer them solid food. The puppies at this stage have very small teeth but will still use the sucking action to eat at first. As described in the previous chapter in the section 'Preparing for the Puppies' Arrival', there are mousse-type foods that come in small, portioned tins; these are ideal as a first food, they reduce waste, and are specially formulated to get puppies on to solids. It's just a case of opening a tin and serving up the contents.

Alternatives are scrambled egg, an instant breakfast porridge-type gruel, and a wheat-biscuit cereal, both softened with warmed goat's milk; make sure these are all cooled to gently warm before feeding. To start with, it is best to serve the food on a flat plate, such as a large pie plate or saucer, as the puppies will not yet know how to reach down for their food. Place them around the plate and take a small tasting on your finger and offer it to each puppy: they should start to suck the food, and if they are ready to eat will be quite eager. Be sure to choose a good quality puppy food, and depending on the type of food, there are different ways of preparing it; just make sure it is completely softened and suitable for baby mouths.

The first few times are quite messy – no, very messy! As the puppies start to taste the new food they usually end up in the dish with it. It is advisable to put a newspaper down with the dish on top, then place the puppies around the dish. Depending on how hungry and ready to eat they are, feeding time will end up in total chaos or a free-for-all! Start by picking up small pieces of food on your finger and offering it to each puppy, and after a few attempts they will then follow your finger down to the food on the plate. This can be repeated each day until they are eating enthusiastically and as demand dictates. Mum will enjoy coming back into the puppies to clean up the dish, and will allow them to finish off with a drink of her milk. However, as the days go by she will start to want to leave the puppies and return to normal life, and eventually she will only return to allow them to drink – at which point you will be feeding them totally.

At this stage it is important to keep an eye on your bitch to make sure her milk supply is waning. As demand drops she will start to dry up, and will soon regain her previous figure. If she continues to make a substantial amount of milk, make sure it is suckled by the puppies, but reduce her visits to the puppy box. Once she is permanently off the puppies, check that her teats have not retained milk – if they become hot and swollen and hard to touch this may be the beginnings of mastitis. If this happens consult your vet as soon as possible.

Whippets are known for their dedication to caring for their puppies, and the bond a mother makes with them can last a lifetime. She can be reluctant to be weaned off her puppies, but often the stampede of numerous mouths with their needle-like teeth on her undercarriage is the deciding factor. Nevertheless she will be happy to visit her puppies and exercise with them as they grow, and you will see her guiding them and teaching them.

Day-To-Day Care

As the puppies grow, their demands will increase and they will enjoy a more solid type of food, so it is probably time to introduce the complete dry type of puppy food. As their teeth are still quite small, soak the nuggets in hot water and allow them to cool. The nuggets will soak up all the water and become soft, and they can be forked into a pulp. This can be used with the mousse or egg, for

As they grow, the puppies still look for reassurance from Mum.

Whippets
have a
special bond
with their
puppies
that lasts a
lifetime.

Even at five
or six weeks
old when
they seem
too big
to suckle,
a drink
is always
welcome.

instance, or on its own. The puppies will soon be eating with gusto and growing very quickly.

To estimate quantity, watch if the puppies eat up the food very quickly and are looking for more, in which case they may need a small increase in the quantity. If they leave a small amount of food, you have probably got it about right. It is very much trial and error. By the time they are fully weaned they will be having four meals a day, with perhaps one as a drink of goat's milk. You should always have a dish of fresh water available for them.

You can allow the puppies to come out of the box to feed on the floor, which you should cover in newspaper; this also encourages them to clean themselves away from their bed. To begin with, their bed will need changing often, as there will be many accidents; mixed with the remains of their dinner, it can get quite dirty quickly. As they eat more, more comes out from the other end, so that makes a considerable amount of faeces from one litter of puppies. It is important to keep an eye out for shyer feeders, those that sit back and let the stronger puppies eat all the food. They may not be quite ready to be enthusiastic about food, but will soon get the idea and join in, or you could provide more than one dish.

Worming

The puppies' first worming should be at around three weeks old. Consult your vet, or a specialist in a good pet store. Worming products can come in a variety of forms such as liquid or paste. These are easy to administer; be sure to follow the instructions for dosage. The next day you should expect to see roundworms in the puppies' faeces. The quantity of worms passed can be quite alarming, but the puppies will then be able to absorb their food, which will promote healthy growth rather than the food they eat feeding worms. Puppies that have a heavy worm infestation can look thin with a hard potbelly, they look unhealthy and pale, and have a 'staring' coat. A bad infestation can result in a painful death.

A regular worming routine should be followed: the manufacturers' instructions or your vet will give guidance. The worms have a cycle that can be broken if the puppies are wormed regularly, and they will then thrive. There is no need to feed expensive puppy food to worms.

Feeding the Growing Puppies

As the puppies progress, you should carry on feeding the appropriate food for their age. There are many specialist formulas for all stages. You can add some fresh meat or tinned puppy food to their diet if you wish. It is useful if they have experienced plenty of varied food before they go to their new homes, as it reduces the chance of their having an upset tummy if their diet is changed. If this does happen, do not repeat that food but go back to their regular food, let their faeces return to normal, then introduce a small amount of the new food and see if it affects them again. It may not be suitable for them. Fresh meat can be ground beef or a small sized, minced green tripe. Fresh meat is always enjoyed enthusiastically, but you may find the green tripe rather smelly!

Socialising

Socialising makes for outgoing puppies. It is ideal if the puppies are in your house as they will see and hear many different things and have constant interaction. If, however, they are kept in an outbuilding or kennel they may need more socialising. A radio is a good way of introducing different sounds and voices, and a variety of toys and items that can be safely used in the puppy pen can be provided to amuse them. However, this is no substitute for spending time with your puppies and giving them human contact so they interact well. Allowing the puppies out of the puppy pen to explore is a good way of allowing them to become more confident and adventurous. However, if children play with them they should be properly supervised. The puppies will love them, but remember they have sharp teeth and claws, and sometimes children can be a little over zealous and if they pick the puppies up, they might then drop them!

Being outdoors introduces a variety of sounds and smells. If the weather is warm, the puppies will thrive in the garden, but it is advisable to use your playpen to prevent them picking up things or ruining your flowering border and emptying your plant pots. They should have drinking water available, and shade if it gets too warm. The main thing is that there is plenty of human contact and encouragement to develop their minds and personalities. Whippet puppies are normally very outgoing, but you may have an individual that is a little more reserved and needs more encouragement.

Exercise

Small puppies are happy to play amongst themselves up to the time they are to leave for their new homes; this is a natural form of exercise and as important as good

The puppies begin to find interesting things in the garden.

Mum still oversees any rowdy behaviour.

Children love puppies and are good at socialising with them, but this should be under strict supervision.

food. All the puppies will benefit from fresh air and sunshine – this is one of the advantages of having a litter in the summer months. They will also sleep quite a lot at this stage, and should be allowed to rest undisturbed. As they grow and get stronger they can be allowed into your garden to run around as detailed above, but to allow too much strenuous exercise can damage their supple bones. Short periods of running around are fine, but no lead training should be started before they are much bigger and in their new homes. As they get to six weeks old, it is possible to put soft collars on them: these come in various colours, are elasticated, and can be easily slipped off if they need removing or get caught on something. This allows the puppies to get used to the feel of a collar, and the different coloured collars are also useful for identifying individual puppies.

Leaving Home

As the breeder of your litter, you have certain decisions to make about your puppies. As they approach the time for leaving home you should consider how you are going to find homes for them. This, of course, should have been a consideration before you even planned the litter, but now the reality is you have a small family that is growing daily and you need to find homes for them. The ideal situation is that homes have already been agreed by word of mouth, but if you are intending to advertise the puppies, you should be planning to start when they are around five to six weeks old. This gives prospective owners the chance to see the puppies before they are ready to go, and decide which puppy is for them. You are now a breeder, and you must decide the best for your own puppies.

Even small puppies play hard and have sharp little needles for teeth.

They grow quickly and soon have long legs.

These puppies show how agile they can be at play.

The puppies should be checked by the vet when they are around six weeks old when their first vaccination is due. This gives both you and the new owners peace of mind. The second vaccination is due at eight weeks old, and at this time your vet will microchip each puppy with its unique code. This is a requirement for all breeders by law. The microchip number is added to the vaccination certificate, and when the new owner takes their puppy, it is registered in their name. The database records the new owner's contact details in case of emergency or if the puppy is lost or stolen.

You should also provide the new puppy owner with a diet sheet, just as you received one when you received your Whippet. Outline the feeding routine and what foods have been used. It is also useful to note the dates of worming, so the new owner can continue the sequence. If your puppies are to be Kennel Club registered you should

have applied for their registration and enclose the certificate for each puppy in your puppy pack. If the certificate hasn't arrived by the time the puppy goes, inform the prospective owner and post it on afterwards.

It is also helpful to advise the new owner before they collect their puppy what food it is eating so they have time to buy some in readiness; alternatively you can give them a small amount when they collect the puppy. It is a good idea to put a small, inexpensive blanket in the puppies' bed for a few days because it takes on their smell, and can go with a puppy when it leaves for its new home: it will comfort a puppy that is suddenly on its own.

You should also be prepared for the eventuality that you are unable to sell your puppies. There is no guarantee of a secure market, and have you the room for an extra four, six or eight Whippets? Are you prepared to take back any of the litter? This is what is expected of a Whippet breeder.

As the breeder of a litter, you never really lose the responsibility of bringing that puppy into the world. Most breeders stipulate that if ever the new owner cannot keep the puppy for whatever reason, it must be returned to them. This alleviates the worry of not knowing where your puppy has ended up, perhaps in a rescue situation or being passed on to another owner who may be unsuitable.

This should be discussed with the new owner, and a contract drafted accordingly. As emphasised before, the breeding of a litter is definitely not a money-making exercise, especially if it is done correctly: it involves hard work, plenty of space, and the costs of food, veterinary fees and equipment – but most of all your time, and this is if it all goes well! Equally, it is very rewarding to breed your own homebred puppy to continue the legacy of your very first Whippet.

Elegance, flowing lines and so beautiful, this stunning photo shows why we love our Whippets.

The Last Word

It may be that luck brings a Whippet into your life, or it may be that your inner self always knew a Whippet would be there. However, it happened, and wherever it led you, only those who have shared their life with Whippets understand the richness they bring in the way of loyalty and companionship, and the sense of pride they generate as they are admired by passers-by. Those passers-by will never know of the stuffing torn out of the cushions, the escape route to the other side of the world in the middle of the lawn, or the inner desire to chase their cat...

Let that be our secret.

Only those who have shared their life with Whippets understand the richness they bring to our lives.

Bibliography

Arrian, Flavius, *Treatise on Hunting* and *Cynegeticus* (c.100AD)

Caius, John, *De Canibus Britannicus* (sixteenth century)

Compton, Herbert, *Twentieth Century Dogs* (1902)

De Sauvenière, A., *Les Courses de Levriers* (1899)

Douglas Todd, C.H., *The Popular Whippet* (1961)

Hignett, F.C., *The New Book of the Dog* (1907)

Lowe, M. and Walsh, E., *The English Whippet* (1984)

Renwick, W. Lewis, *The Whippet Handbook* (1957)

Shaw, Vero, *The Illustrated Book of the Dog* (1879)

Contacts

The Kennel Club: www.thekennelclub.org.uk

JR Whippet Rescue www.whippetrescue.org.uk

Index

Other Titles from Crowood

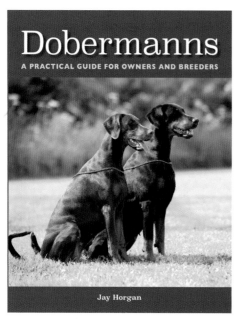

978 1 78500 308 0

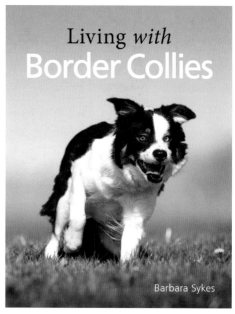

978 1 78500 981 5

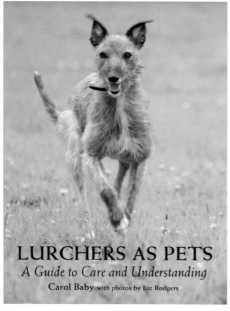

978 1 84797 911 7

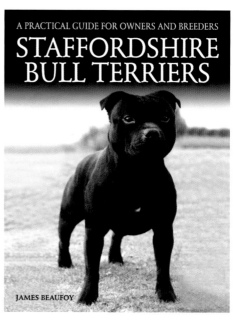

978 1 78500 096 6